Books by John Gould

NEW ENGLAND TOWN MEETING

PRE-NATAL CARE FOR FATHERS

FARMER TAKES A WIFE

THE HOUSE THAT JACOB BUILT

AND ONE TO GROW ON

NEITHER HAY NOR GRASS

MONSTROUS DEPRAVITY

PARABLES OF PETER PARTOUT

YOU SHOULD START SOONER

THE FASTEST HOUND DOG IN THE STATE OF MAINE

(WITH F. WENDEROTH SAUNDERS)

YOU SHOULD
START SOONER

YOU SHOULD
START SOONER

In which widely separated topics are strangely discussed by an old cuss.

by JOHN GOULD

I find it ain't always so much what a man says — it's a question of what he means when he says it. — PETER PARTOUT

with illustrations by
F. WENDEROTH SAUNDERS

Little, Brown and Company · Boston · Toronto

The essays herein originally appeared in the *Christian
Science Monitor*, under "A Dispatch from the Farm" on
the editorial page.

*Published simultaneously in Canada
by Little, Brown & Company (Canada) Limited*

PRINTED IN THE UNITED STATES OF AMERICA

Dedicated to

JAY FEIN
D. D. GURNEE
BROWNLEE HAYDON
AND OTHERS.

****

Dear John:

Whatever happened to my suggestion that the *CSM* collect Gould in book form?

BROWNLEE HAYDON

To the *Christian Science Monitor*:

Please advise me as to when, Oh when, either you or someone else is going to publish a book containing a collection of those priceless writings of John Gould's which have been appearing in your paper for so long? If they are not yet published, it is high time someone woke up and did the job. They are the most Americanlike things appearing in any paper today.

D. D. GURNEE

Mr. Gould:

Have your "Dispatch from the Farm" articles ever been compiled, and if so in what publication can they be found?

JAY FEIN

The Dispatch from the Farm

Something like 1100 essays ago, the editor of the *Christian Science Monitor* wrote to tell me that the editorial staff was pondering on the best way to present my essays to the readership. They settled, shortly, on what the sanctum calls the "fifth column" — the center of the editorial page just under the daily cartoon.

Since then, many readers have suggested a collection of these weekly dispatches in a book. Here is that book. I offer it somewhat as a record of a happy career in journalism. The selections are my own.

JOHN GOULD

Lisbon Falls, Maine

INTRODUCTION

Now I will confess. I will tell you how it came about that John Gould's Dispatches from the Farm were first published in the *Christian Science Monitor*. John knows. He does not find the story very funny. Neither do I.

When I was a little boy, we lived on a farm in Lisbon, Maine, only a couple of miles away from the Gould homestead, now made famous by John's delightful prose. John was lots younger than I am. I never knew him then.

But I knew his grandfather, Tom Gould. He drove his horse and buggy up and down the road past our farm at least once a week. He drove to Lewiston carrying whatever produce he had to sell, and drove back with whatever he could buy for it. I suspect it wasn't very much. He was a craggy, gnarled old boy. My grandfather played checkers and disputed with Tom sometimes. He referred to him often as one of the village characters. In 1917, I remember, Tom opposed Woodrow Wilson's war. "Old Tom Gould is talking like a copperhead these days," said my grandfather, who was no fire-breathing patriot himself.

Anyway, one nice summer's day I was playing in our yard. Mr. Gould had already driven up the road toward Lewiston. Down the road came the Banana Man. This was an itinerant peddler, with a bony horse and ramshackle cart. He drove down the road selling exotic fruits, like oranges and bananas, and drove back with a load of rags, bottles, and junk. On this day, my grandmother or mother bought a hand of bananas and I begged one.

I took the banana out by the road. I didn't eat it at once. A Maine boy didn't. It was too rare a treat. I slit the banana peel with my finger nail, extracted the banana in one piece, and ate it with little bites, savoring every taste. I still had the peel, also in one piece, looking like a complete banana.

The devil entered me. I took the booby banana out into the road and laid it down in the dusty wheel-track, to deceive who might come by. Then I hid in the bushes. Sure enough, a horse and buggy came down the road. It was driven by Tom Gould, coming back from Lewiston. The poor old horse's head hung low. He was tired, and so was Tom. But his countryman's eye spied the banana in the road. He undoubtedly thought the Banana Man had dropped it, and hope must have sprung up in his weary heart. He drew the horse to a stop, cramped the front wheels, painfully stepped down from the seat, and walked ahead to the banana. He picked it up. Then only did he perceive the hoax. With an air of infinite disillusionment, tired, hot, hungry, thirsty, disappointed again by life's vagrant hope and promise, he climbed back into the buggy and drove home.

My heart burned within me. I was so sorry. Poor Mr. Gould. How sad he had looked. What a wicked thing I had done. But what could I do about it? Nothing. *Then.*

Thirty years later, a manuscript signed by John Gould reached the offices of the *Christian Science Monitor.* We had already known of John as a kind of press officer for Goddard College in Vermont. But we didn't know he was a light essayist. His very first piece, I must say, was extremely good. Even if it hadn't been, the then managing editor would have tried awfully hard to find some way to print it. But there was no need to try.

And now, nearly twenty-five years later, the Dispatches From the Farm come together in this delightful volume. I am glad that the *Monitor*'s readers have liked them as well as the editor has, and without any of his conscientious compulsions. Now a wider audience has its chance to savor them. They preserve memories and values which are a rich element in American life. They have a part to play in the future of a good society.

I can still taste that banana, and it tastes better now than it did after Tom Gould let the peel fall in the dust. John has paid the debt to Tom far better than I could, but I'm glad I had a small part in it.

Erwin D. Canham
Editor in Chief
Christian Science Monitor

YOU SHOULD
START SOONER

YOU SHOULD START SOONER

The gay yellow school buses do not make their appointed rounds if the highway crew has not first cleared new-fallen snow. So if a plow breaks down there is no school. On a morning when the new snow is deep and you can sit in a rocker in the kitchen with the cat on your knees, there is time for both you and the cat to meditate quietly, and just now I got to thinking about the time I got buried in the cowshed. Just such a storm as this, and I was late for school.

We'd already had some good storms that winter, and this one I mention added a couple more feet. It was enough, too, to demonstrate a flaw in our architecture, because we'd hung the cowshed door so it swung out. In the snow belt of Maine, this is silly, and I don't know how we came to do it. We'd widened the shed that summer, added some windows, and thought we'd done well.

[3]

When I came down into the kitchen that morning snow covered the windows, so Mother had a lamp burning as she stirred the porridge at the stove. Upstairs, there had been the noise of the wind and the driving flakes, but here in the kitchen there was no sound of the welter outside. Insulated against noise, cold and light, we were snug as any Eskimo, and I pulled on my storm clothes and made ready for my morning trek to chore the cow.

I wasn't a six-footer then, and the drifts were. I slung the milk pail over one elbow, clutched a turned-down barn lantern in that hand, and held the big wooden snow shovel in the other. So I wallowed to the shed, and it wasn't easy. I dug down, clearing snow until the door would swing, and as soon as it swung enough I squeezed in. It took more room for the fourteen-quart milk pail than it did for me. I made it, pulled the door to, and shot the hasp.

My black cow, usually up and eager at the first sound of approaching breakfast, was not ready for me that morning. The snow had covered her windows, too, and she had no warning that morning had come. As far as she knew it was still last night. Abruptly, some intruder had violated her boudoir and surprised her. She started to get up just as I squeezed through the door.

A cow, you know, gets up hind-end foremost. It

[4]

is an anatomical maneuver least designed to accommodate the style of manger in which man usually installs her. When she is down, her head stretched forward on her grain box and her great body relaxed in the sweet comfort of repose, she would do a lot better to stand up front-end first. This would save her from ramming her snout into the boards, and the whole manipulation would be more congenial. But instead, she hoists her stern aloft, and for the partial elevation thus gained she pays dearly on the bow. Given sufficient time to awake, shake off drowsiness, and do the thing with dignity and poise, a cow can make out, but when an element of urgency or surprise is added she goes all to pieces.

My cow then went to pieces. Suddenly intruded upon, she came to with a jerk and began to stand up. By the time she had her hind quarters at a point, I had closed the door behind me and with her head in the feed box she decided whatever it was she had been mistaken. Neither up nor down, she stood there deciding if she had heard something or not, and at last she decided she had not and began to recline her posterior again. But just then I turned up the wick in the lantern and bathed the tie-up in the yellow kerosene glow.

This convinced her it was morning so she shifted to rise again. But I suppose she knew that lanterns were

[5]

for night, not morning, and she went back to bed. Her thought processes then went to pot entirely, and I stood there in the shed and watched the stern end of my cow rising and lowering, rising and lowering, so confused she was that dusk or dawn she wotted not.

I go into details, because all this took a lot of time, and time is of the essence. When at last I spoke to her she responded, engaging her coordination, and she got the front end up the next time the hind end went by, and she turned to look at me with sad brown eyes, asking mutely how all this started, anyway. I brushed her down, speaking cajolingly as is the proper approach, but she was taut and distraught as I milked her, her ears laid back and her eyes bugged.

A cow, thus wound up, usually becomes a "hard" milker, and it takes longer than usual to drain her. At that time she was filling the pail, foam and all, to about an inch from the top, and I worried about toting that heft of splashing milk through the new snow back to the house. Indeed, this same consideration had decided me against watering her that morning, for in winter we lugged her beverage in pails from the house. I could let that go until after school. But she stripped out at last, I filled her crib with hay, and there I was.

It had taken so long that the snow had blown back against the door, and I was trapped by an outswinging portal in snow country. There wasn't a thing I could do except wait to be saved. Mother, busy with bacon and eggs and feeding and dressing the other children, would think of me in time, and after she pulled on some heavy clothes would come out to see why I was detained. The froth on my pail of milk had settled completely by the time she did this, and the cream had started to rise. I heard her call to me through the door, and then she began digging away the snow.

We didn't get bussed to school in those times, and we all went to school that morning — I was on ahead breaking a path for my brothers and sisters. We were all late, and my teacher asked me how that happened. I told her about the cow and the driving snow, and she said on bad mornings I ought to start sooner.

OF PRIMING AND PUMPING

Fraser, Colorado, appears now to be a fake. I can't find it in Webster's Geographical Dictionary, and during the past cold spell its well-established reputation as a television weatherman's horrible example was completely exploded. I just came into the house from a genial State of Maine 38-below to find the man on Channel 8 telling me Fraser was the nation's coldest spot with a minus 22. I am typing this with my mittens on, and thus the winter wanes away.

During this spell of weather Fraser has been getting hotter and hotter, and we have been losing ground, and old timers say this is as bad as we've ever had. I have not tried to start my automobile, so I don't have any opinions backed by modern measurements.

Nowadays a drop in temperature is important only as it affects getting the family vehicle going, and the conversational appurtenances thereto are manifold. A man whose conveyance chugs off immediately becomes something of a neighborhood hero and he brags. He gives a push to his friends and makes fun of their models, and becomes objectionable. When it warmed up to 18-below one morning last week we thought the worst was over.

Somehow these cool mornings make me think of priming a pump. Back when F.D.R. began talking about priming the pump for political purposes I used to have a little fun asking his warmer supporters if they knew what he meant. I used to wonder if he did. Today you can telephone from a comfortable kitchen and have the garage man come and start your automobile nicely, but starting the old barn pump was something you did yourself. During a cold spell like this one there was little about it which suggested national political dimensions, and the fact that I knew about "pump priming" was reason enough to hold aloof from the New Deal. Only those who never primed a pump would subscribe.

A pump was made, in its chamber, so when you lifted the handle high it would trigger a release, and the water would drain back in the well. In winter weather you always did this after gaining what water you needed, otherwise the freeze-up would burst the pump and the pipe; at least would cement the handle motionless. Since every family includes at least one muddle-headed member who might forget to lift the handle high for a moment, farmers had a way of making this automatic. They would take the plunger out of the pump, and cut a little notch in the leather. The notch wasn't big enough to hamper the suction when you were pumping, but it was big enough to let the water run down before it froze. Then if somebody forgot to lift on the handle, the water would leak by itself with a gasping, gurgling, prolonged hissing until all was safe.

Then the pump would cool all night. Even though most of the water drained down, there was always enough moisture to form frost, and this glued things together inside. The leathers would freeze and become crisp. And then I would arise in the brisk dawn and go down to the barn and prime that pump until it drew water again, and all the thirsty animals could get a drink. This chore began the night before, when you set a pail of water close to the stove in the kitchen. This water was for priming. Then we would take our hot bricks from the oven, wrap them in flannel, and run to our beds up in the unheated chambers. We pushed the bricks down into the cold sheets to warm our feet. The air in one of our bedrooms was just as cold and fresh whether you opened a window or not. We liked the solid weight of blankets and comf-tibles, and we snuggled in to shiver until we got warm. During the night we could listen to the nails pulling.

Unless you remember nails pulling in the roof on a winter night, you shouldn't be talking about cold weather. The air would be still as a pirate's conscience, the stars close down with their cut-glass edges sharp and blue, and a fox snarling three miles away would seem to be right under the window. Somehow all this built up a stress in the construction, and up in the roofers an old hand-wrought nail would pop out. It sounded like a pistol shot, closer than any sonic boom, and deep down under your bedding you would come awake in a twitch and think about that old pump in the barn and the inevitable morning.

Once in a while the hardwood fire in the kitchen range would burn down sooner than usual, and the pail of water would freeze. Sometimes during the night the very heart of the home would drop below 32°, and the priming water turned to ice. Then you had to get the fire going again, wait until you had heat enough to thaw the pail. There was always something about the benefits of political pump priming that sounded harsh and out of tune to an old pump primer from away back who could freeze a pail of water on his kitchen floor. This was never my idea of the way to start prosperity.

Then to the barn with a pail that cast steam into the air, and the waking cattle would stand up and adjust to their stanchions, and turn to watch you with their big brown eyes. No maestro ever raised his baton before as critical an audience. In their silent gaze was utter contempt for anybody put to priming a pump. The dry, cold, ice-crusted interior of the pump barrel snapped when the first warm water was poured in, and the limber handle was futile in its search for water. It took a long time. But as the metal lost its frost and the leathers became pliant again, there was eventually a different sound and the suction began to build up. The cattle were placid at first, but when they could hear water coming up in the pipe they began to stir, and some of them would low their approval.

Afterwards they were released two at a time and pumping continued until all had their drinks. Pumping worked up a sweat, but it was nothing like the sweat that might come to you later that morning in school, when in geography or history your thoughts wandered, and you couldn't remember if you let the pump down or not.

No, I haven't tried to start my automobile this cold spell, and the days of priming a winter pump are gone. But if there is any Fraser, Colorado, and they think it's cold there, I'm not impressed.

PHEASANTS ON THE LOOSE

The second day of October, falling on a Monday, turned out to be the opening of the bird season — which I had neglected to mark down as such and so fared forth briskly in the beauty of the dawn as if 'twere any other lovely day. And it so happened that my thoughts turned upon a pear for breakfast, which makes the second of October about right, and I thought if I got one I would cut it up into pieces and eat it out of a nappy with some sugar on it.

I would state that as far as birds go I am in a special situation. Our upland acres are pleasant and congenial, and birds like to live here. And we have in Maine a game-management program which culminates about September when all the game wardens come around with trucks loaded with crates and turn ring-necked pheasants loose. These birds are hatched and grown on a game farm, so-called, and are pawns in the "put and take" policy of the sporting program. The pheasant originated in Asia, back in the Ding-Dong Dynasty somewhere, and has been a domesticated bird ever since. He is no more wild than a Barred Rock pullet, or a hired girl going to the woodpile for kindlings. But after he is spoonfed all summer, he is taken into the back country and released, and by legislative fiat he is now "wild." He is game. He is also a nuisance around a farm and will peck the crops. One year when it was dry and they were seeking moisture they ruined about a thousand bushels of my Yellow Delicious apples, right on the boughs.

I disposed of them, that year, before the season opened. I am a good shot with the varmint gun, and shooting pheasants proved to be about as sporty as trapping mice in a pantry. I dressed them out, wrapped them well, and put them in the freezer. Then I told the game warden what I had done, and I showed him a beautiful yellow apple with the side gone from it. "You can't do that!" he said. I said I had already done it, and if he wanted the pheasants he could come and get them. I also told him that if he ever released any more pheasants on my land I'd shoot him.

But it doesn't matter much where they let them go. The land lies so the pheasants released all up and down the valley work up onto me. The reason they have introduced the pheasant as a game bird is to take the "pressure" off pa'tridges (ruffed grouse) and woodcock. These birds can't be hatched and nurtured in a hen-pen, and as more and more people take up gunning the state needed to find something for them to gun. The agile hunter can shoot pheasants right from his automobile seat, and this is dandy.

So we don't see a pheasant from snow-go to August, but suddenly all the crates are unbuttoned and the fields swarm with pheasants. By the last week in September we'll see fifteen or twenty eating holly-hock seeds by the back door; they roost at night in the flowering crab on the front lawn, and they set our barnyard mallards into a tizzy by stealing their mash at the hopper. I suppose they don't know (and I forgot) that October is open season, and that how-ever tame they may be tonight, they are legally wild

[14]

tomorrow. So as I say, I arose thinking pear, and I pulled on my rubber boots against the heavy dew of the morn and sallied forth to my pear tree.

It was a lovely dawn and every prospect pleased. The catbird and cuckoo called cheerily from the glen, and a raucous crow answered forsooth from yonder pine. The mists of the morning hung over the east'ard valley and the sun was working on them with a will. The bay of a tied-up hound over in the next town sounded mournful and distressed. Beads of dew festooned the thistle and the gorse, whatever gorse is, and my pantslegs were soon soaked above my boots. It was refreshing, clean and beautiful. To pop from bed into the magnificence of a country morning remains one of life's finest joys, and to have a nice ripe pear on top of that is almost more than mortal deserves.

The pear tree I had in mind, and which I have since picked, is an understanding tree that cooperates fully. It knows that no pear is any good until it has yellowed on the twig and dropped into the dew-drenched dawn just in time for breakfast. It was my thought to show appreciation of this bounty, and be there to catch such a pear on the first bounce. Thus I was oriented pearwise and, absorbed by the peripheral peace and loveliness, approached the tree without anything else on my mind.

About seventeen feet beyond the barn, therefore, I almost stepped on a cock pheasant in the grass, and rudely interrupted his matutinal meditations. He made a long outcry, after his kind, which is something like having a John Peel obligato blown in your ear by a mad bugler, and at this a whole flock of bedded-down pheasants arose from the grass all about me and flew off in thirty-eight directions. Nor did I know that five lusty hunters, assisted by two fine bird dogs, had been creeping up on this lair from the morning mists beyond.

Before I could retreat I had been decimated by twenty-seven shots, each of which hissed past me distinctly enough so I counted each and every one separately. None actually struck me, and I am happy to report that none struck a pheasant, either. The gentlemen, having discharged their weapons, then indicated they were put out because I had flushed the covey before they were ready. They seemed to think a householder going after a morning pear should gear himself to the sporting possibilities, and have greater respect for the amenities.

Thinking the Battle of Gettysburg was being re-enacted by the National Guard, my wife arose during the volley, and our old dog, who is gun-shy, went under the refrigerator. When I came into the kitchen, feeling like Pershing on a triumphal return from the front, she said, "I forgot all about the hunting season!"

The pear was delicious.

LEFT-HAND NUTS

After long resistance I bought me a chainsaw. I haven't paid for it yet, so I'm lucky, but things have gone about as I expected. Well, you see, I don't cut much wood any more, and the noise of a chainsaw in my woods would seem like an intrusion on a sturdy past. But sentiment fades before the inroads of the era of comfort and ease, and noisy as it is a chainsaw will do quite a chore. And some of my reluctance to go modern was born of an observation that men with chainsaws spend a great deal of time fixing them.

This pertains to a common fault in the whole agricultural area. Machinery, implements and devices turned out for farmers have a margin of error you could drive a team of horses through with a ladder on crosswise. A nation smart enough to start a rocket toward the moon ought to be able to make a chainsaw that will work, or a cutterbar that will mow grass. Alas. The raucous whine of the chainsaw on the

[17]

morning air, assaulting the peace of the lovely bucolic scene, suddenly stops and you know the man is adjusting his tension again.

Tractors, cultivators, water pumps, milking machines — all such have a factor of desuetude, and I'm sure if the American farmer could get equipment that would work he'd do his sixteen-hour day in banker's time. But the other day I had a chance, so I dickered for a chainsaw, and I explained to the man that I was not a lumberman and didn't own a pulpmill. My needs were moderate, and if I could get something reliable that would limb a tree and keep my fireplace and shop stove going I would be glad.

I pointed out that this didn't warrant the long price on a new saw (they cost more than they should, anyway), but if I could get something that would start when I pulled the string and would run until I was tuckered the need would be served. Least of all, I said, I didn't want any transaction to lead to the constant going and coming to the repair shop that seemed standard for the trade. "There are more chainsaws being repaired in dealers' back rooms than there are in the Maine woods," I said, looking behind him at the broken chainsaws he had piled up.

He said he knew just what I meant, and that he had a beauty. "This one will cut like going through butter," he said. "When you pull the string it's just like unlacing a shoe." He said it was just the checker, and he was glad to see me have it because he was partial to it and wanted it to have a good home that didn't keep late hours. I took it home, a little pleased that my character was strong enough to make this change from a sentimental past.

The next morning I made ready for a day in the woods. I mixed oil with gasoline, got down the box of wrenches. I laid in the ax and peavey, the big maul and the wedges. I took a lunch. The tractor drew the trailer up across the fields, crunching on the rime-frost of the morning, and I drove down into the woods to stop by a big beech that I had in mind. I parked the rig so it wouldn't be under the tree when it came down. I took the ax and cleared the brush away so my footing was clear. And I found the man had told me the truth — just like unlacing a shoe, and when I jerked the struggle-string the engine roared after its kind. Clean-cut explosions from the spark indicated perfect carburetion and correct adjustment throughout. It was a joyful sound, and I could see that this was a fine saw. It continued to run in this highly excellent fashion for three seconds, going on four, and then it leaped into the air about a foot and fell to the ground to lie silent in the woodland dell. A beautiful peace fell over the countryside, and I could hear the beech leaves rustling in the bright northish wind that was also flapping my ears.

This bright northish wind is not the best company while you are dissecting a chainsaw on a frozen stump and trying to find out what slew it. It seemed to me the recoil mechanism had got mixed with the rudder, somehow, and when you have mittens on a three-sixteenth isn't too different from a seven-thirty-second. I found my thoughts turning on the chainsaw man, who had a warm shop and a congenial bench, with his tools all handy, and who had said "Eyah, sure!" when I spoke of all the chainsaws he had in for repairs. I turned the tractor around and gave my chainsaw a nice ride home, and then I took it to his warm shop and gave it back to him. "That's funny," he said. "Not ha-ha, but tch-tch." "Eyah, sure," I said.

I said it was a funny country that can make an astronaut circle the globe three times, but can't make a chainsaw. He said she'd cut or he'd know the reason why. He spent the next few hours knowing the reason why.

I think I know why. There's a left-hand nut. I've always been leery of left-hand nuts. When the struggle-string disengages and the flywheel takes over, this nut comes loose. Mechanics tell us it isn't supposed to, and it is a left-hand nut so it won't. I think anything that requires a left-hand nut is basically unsound. Billions have been spent on solid fuels for intercontinental missiles, but technology has never spent fifteen cents' worth of thought on the absurdity of left-hand nuts.

To date, my chainsaw has not spewed one scrid of sawdust and has yet to ease my burden in the woodlot. The man has repeatedly "fixed" it, and I have repeatedly carried it home and brought it back. It sits now in the shop, waiting for me to try again, and I'm trying to talk myself into it. All the time I meant to spend sawing, my fuel has been put into caddying a chainsaw, and I think this is about par for the course.

I do keep congratulating myself that I haven't paid for it yet.

PAUSING PAWS

Every time I have tried to offer invaluable observations on the pussy cat as a responsible member of the social order, it turns out that the cat has more friends than I do. You will therefore notice considerable reluctance on my part to push the subject and be downright. Cats, I have found, come in numerous sorts, few of which appeal to me and lots of which do not. I know some people like that, too.

I have, myself, a lovely cat, a magnificent Manx beast who sticks two inches of pins in my knee to show her affection, and probably would look the other way if the bank foreclosed and only her prompt attention would save me from ruin. It occurs to me that the cat who walks alone, and to whom all places are the same, observes one important exception to this quotation. A cat does not like to walk through a doorway, and the other side of the door is not the same. A great deal of the cat business lies in a category where I can do nothing, but this door problem is my meat. My great success in training my stub-tailed cat to pass through a door rapidly and without hesitation deserves more than casual notice.

A cat, full of new milk and venom, about to pass from the kitchen into the broad outdoors where adventure calls, follows a set cat pattern. I have noticed this in all cats I have been privileged to watch. They skulk along the woodwork and approach the egress gingerly. They will hang back and hang back, and then trot the last four feet to the threshold as if they were going to sail out by. But then they stop, and they look out and wait, and look out and stay there. The owner of said cat then spends his time waiting for said cat to make up his or her mind, so-called. Anybody who has a cat thus spends a good time at the door waiting for something to happen, door open and everything ready.

My Stubbie meows when she wants out, a lingering howl of insolence which solidifies the marrow and tingles the spine.

And this always happens at the wrong time. I'm always doing something else that is not geared to opening a door for a cat. I may just be full of supper, sitting on the back of my neck in the rocker with my feet up, and not caring about cats or anything. I may be standing up on a stool, hanging a bag of grape jelly to drip. Stubbie has never yet wanted out if anybody is handy and available. If I'm adding up figures or counting something, that's for Stubbie. So I used to interrupt my preoccupation or my activity, and I'd go and open the door for Stubbie, and then the two of us would stand there and she'd look out.

This goes back to the jungle, no doubt. Caution. Look before you leap. Mistrust everything. Who knows what dire surprise might be out there? There might even be a cat trap.

Our dooryard has been Stubbie's for eleven good years. If there is anything there now which she doesn't know about, it's late in the game to discover it. She's perfectly capable of taking care of herself anyway, and once she rode a Great Dane down the road, getting off lightly just this side of the next house to allow the dog to keep going another mile.

So, because it seemed to me this caution was misplaced, I assisted Stubbie one morning when she was young by prodding her with my boot. I don't mean an old swingeroo, but a gentle nudge. It infiltrated, sort of, and as her thoughts were on a possible forward danger it astonished her by coming from behind. She embraced a forward alacrity at this invasion of her privacy, and she cleared the petunia bed by three feet and went under the roses like a dart from a blowgun. I had so much success with this that I did it five or six times, but after that Stubbie was conditioned and I was never fast enough to do it again. Stubbie became one of the few cats in the cat business who dallied not upon a threshold.

This is a wonderful thing to teach a cat. And it works both ways. If I am coming in with my arms loaded with firewood or berry baskets she may knock me off my feet as she passes through, but she dillies not. She leaps through and slides across the linoleum and up against the far wall, but she comes in. She has to pick herself up and recover her dignity, but this is not hard for a cat, and then she will investigate the dog's dish to see if he missed anything and let on nothing happened.

A quick-passing cat is a great saving on heating

bills. A reluctant cat, monopolizing the doorway, can let the wind in until it hoists books off tables and the thermostat in the front hall clicks like castanets. But Stubbie hasn't turned on a thermostat in ten years.

The other end of this story is that her abbreviated, or Manx, tail permits rapid closing of the portal afterwards. On regular cats you have to wait until the tail goes by. With Stubbie her instantaneous transition is a good thing. It isn't catlike, but it can be induced.

This is the only cat habit I have ever tried to do anything about. Stubbie is normal otherwise. She carries on loud and lengthy conversations under my window with other cats, and so on, but I just let those things go. But I like the carefree way a dog bounds through a doorway, and I thought a cat should be taught the wisdom of this. They learn quickly, if you start early and keep at it. The other side of a cat's door can become as any other place. You may get a dirty look from your cat for a while, but she gets over it. From most cats, you get that anyway.

TRUNKS, TRAINS AND TV

Everybody used to have a trunk. I had one, even, and I didn't go anywhere. The extinction

[25]

of the trunk, as an adjunct of American civilization, occurred to me just now as I was looking for some sugar skimmers in the attic, and I had to climb over a trunk that belonged to Aunt Harriet. Maybe it was Cousin Harriet. Anyway, she flourished in a bygone era with enough style so she remains a family tradition, and I never knew anybody who set eyes on her. We mention her occasionally: "Use Aunt Harriet's pickle dish!" they'll say in the kitchen when they're turning out relish for the beans. So she remains in mind, but her empty trunk back under the eaves in the attic serves now only to remind us about the inadequacies of modern television.

Well, in these period plays that we see on our screens, the modern morality of virtue triumphant, we now and then have the pleasure of seeing an old-time American railroad station. Here in Maine, where railroad passenger service was long since discontinued, this is a treat. Everybody likes trains. If the entertainment industry is going to maintain historical railroad equipment for photographic and broadcast purposes, I think they should get some trunks like Aunt Harriet's. Because I don't remember, in any of these plays, seeing proper emphasis on the trunk activity around the baggage car. And it wasn't thus. Whenever you went anywhere you took a trunk, and as you

coursed a "depot" platform you had to dodge expressmen pulling on their hand wagons of trunks.

We had a family uncle, and he was in my time,
who regularly made train trips between here and
"out West," and he never came or went without his
trunk. I don't know what happened on the far end
of his travels, but on this end we'd meet him with
the buggie or pung and lash his trunk behind with
what he called a rope but we called a line. Then we'd
drive up to the farm and he'd stay with us for a
time. After he had enough of us he'd pack up, and
we'd drive him to the station and watch Herman
Ogilvie shove the trunk into the baggage car.

Trunks were checked. You bought your ticket,
and then you would go to the baggage window and
the man would punch your ticket in a little square,
indicating baggage traveled with you. The railroads,
fully justifying the ancient criticism that they didn't
think much of the public, seldom kept the traveler's
trunk in context. You would arrive at your destina-
tion, but your trunk usually came on a later train —
and this is an important part of transportation history
in this country. Take Boston, for instance — in all
the years of efficient rail travel, they never fixed it so
a passenger could ride through Boston. My uncle,
coming from Dakota to Maine, would come into

[27]

Boston on one train, getting off at the South Station. Then he would have to take the subway or a hack and cross the city to the North Station, where another railroad would bring him to Maine. His trunk, meantime, would go by way of Providence, Worcester, Lawrence and assorted way stations and seldom arrived at our little local depot at the same time he did. Many times we'd see Herman Ogilvie at the Farmers' Union and he'd say, "Your uncle is coming, his trunk got in today on No. 5." Other times we'd meet Uncle, and then go back two days later to get his trunk.

We still have his trunk. It is a massive thing all brassbound and cornered, and it has a rounded top. The domed top on a trunk was to discourage stacking them, so expressmen couldn't pile one on another until the bottom one got crushed. The traveling public would sit in the coaches believing their trunks were all on the floor, but the expressmen simply stood them on end and stacked them that way. A good expressman could stack anything.

The trunk couldn't travel today, on buses or planes. And its eye-appeal wouldn't please; the trunk is so thoroughly outdated nobody would be seen with one.

Here in Maine with our coastal customs we had a sea-going version of the overland trunk. The sea

chest. It still has an attraction, and while trunks languish in attics the sea chest is admired as a household antique. We've got a couple of them, left over from many voyages. They are pine chests, beautifully dovetailed, with hemp beckets and wrought-iron hinges and locks. Even now, after many years of being used for blanket chests, if you open one on a warm day you'll get a whiff of tars and spices from the far places of the world.

No seafaring man ever took a trunk or a "dress-suitcase" aboard ship. Passengers did, but to a mariner this was sometimes held unlucky. The seaman had a bag, a diddy box and a chest. (Some folklorist might like to know that in Maine you don't hear the term suitcase — it is dress-suitcase, in full.) Another companion for the trunk was the grip, which seems to be a contraction of gripsack — it had handles for gripping. In this you toted things you might need on the trip. Uncle's grip was a handsome piece of leather and an addition to any railway platform. I remember once he was putting in some chicken sandwiches to sustain him while traveling, and when he opened it I saw two pearl-handled Colt .45 revolvers on top of his shirts. That's the closest I ever came to the rip-snorting days of Leadville, Laramie and the like.

Because of the seafaring of old Maine, an attic will

now and then have an exotic trunk, and one such was the hairy trunk. It would be covered with camel skin, with the fur still on it. This was really class. Anybody going ashore in a port of call, to stay a night or two in a hotel, would cut quite a figure with his hairy trunk. But when stored in Maine attics a generation or so this camel hair lost its sheen, and the trunk would bedraggle. Thus came the term, "a bald-headed trunk."

There was one old yarn about a lady who was herself thinning out on top, and when she applied some hair restorer her hand slipped and she spilt some on her trunk. Every so often she'd have to take her trunk to the barber's for a haircut.

Our old trunks didn't open out into a room or an apartment, either. They didn't have spare rooms with shelves and drawers. They had a lift lid and then a tray which came out. Uncle kept his clothing down in the trunk, but used the tray for his souvenirs and valuables. A little box for collar buttons, his Bible and his "Bluebook." Papers, one of which was a government deed to a quarter section in "Dakotah Territory." Whatever Uncle had, it was in that trunk, and the trunk is still there as he left it. Aunt Harriet, on the other hand, left a trunk which is still empty. She never made a trip beyond the Grange Hall, but she had a trunk.

BLUEBERRY BLUES

In midsummer came a breathless courier of the United States Mails with an urgent communication from a young woman in Boston, hitherto a stranger. She inquired if I could tell her a good place to catch blueberries. Maine is the greatest blueberry country in the world, and I am a keen student of the ripened product. I know where the blueberry lurks. So there was no problem, except that a sly thought crept into my agile mind, and I wondered if . . .

Well, you see, there are two kinds of blueberries, as far as I'm concerned. One is the native, low-bush, wild Maine blueberry that we rake by the thousands of tons and can or freeze for the trade. We burn over the long fields to prune the bushes, and harvest them in a tumult of activity that produces good cash. Ever since I was a boy in high school and first studied the mythology of Greece, I have wondered why the immortal gods sat on Olympus eating nectar and ambrosia when they could have moved to Mt. Katahdin and had blueberry pie. Ever since I was a boy I have gone forth in season and gathered these delectables, and although I get a lot we never have too many.

The other kind of blueberry is the "high-bush,"

which is derived from a fruit nursery. This young woman in Boston said that she knew nothing about blueberries but wanted to become acquainted. I knew nothing about high-bush blueberries, and I got acquainted. In the catalog the item gets high praise. "One plant is enough for a family," it says, showing a colored photograph of clusters of bright blue fruit with the dew on them. Since nursery catalogs always come in February, which is the low point of the year, they have an advantage in creating desire. It is much easier, in February, to separate a Maine farmer from his money in the fruit department. Being ardent about blueberries, I succumbed. I bought a dozen high-bush blueberry plants, and they are doing fine out back of the barn in a good place. The last time I walked that way they were hung with berries just as the catalog said they would be. My thought was that I would take the young woman from Boston out there and turn her loose. If she doesn't know anything about blueberries . . .

When those plants came that spring I carefully set them with the highest expectation. It seemed impossible that the tiny shoots, carefully cut back by the nursery, would quickly sprout into exuberant bushes, to give me mammoth great blueberries that would look like those in the picture. That gorgeous blue was a high spot in the graphic arts, and I smiled to think anybody might make a pie from half a blueberry. (Well, in the domestic science classes in school the girls make cookies with a quarter of an egg. This allows four girls to be graduated on one egg, no matter how sombre the cookies.)

The bushes did well. I kept an eye on them. They spent two years waxing, and on the third spring they put out gobs of buds that were as good as a license to steal. These developed into green berries until the tips turned down. I could see that the hyperbolic advertising was indeed discreet and restrained. I could see what "festoon" means.

Then I went and bought a box of rubber balloons. I blew them up and tied them to stakes around the blueberry plants so they'd bob around in the breeze. This was to frighten away predatory birds, like robins. Each day I would go out and rearrange the balloons, so the birds wouldn't grow accustomed to them in one location, thus creating an illusion of numbers like an early settler shooting Indians from six loopholes at once. It worked, too. Not a bird picked a berry, and one day the blueberries were all blue and the harvest was at hand.

I picked a pailful, and then got another pail. I filled a tub and was half-way up a hogshead. You never saw such berries. Each was as big as a marble and ripe as a soft grape. I arranged the crop in pint baskets and lined them up on my roadside stand. "They sell on sight," the catalog had said, and this proved to be true. Tourists squealed their brakes and dragged to a stop. At fifty cents a pint I was soon rolling in wealth. Even some of my neighbors, who have wild blueberries by the acre, stopped to try a box. I contemplated investing in more bushes, perhaps putting the upper ten-acre field into blueberries from the nursery, and I could see myself retiring as a blueberry king.

The next morning we all had a dish of these delectable berries for breakfast, and the dream of empire faded. A great howl went up from my family. "Do I have to eat these!" somebody wailed, and I could just barely make out the words for the shriveled tongue and puckered lips.

I won't say they were sour, because that's a word we use for pickles, but they were not up to the standards of the ordinary wild blueberry of my youth. I wouldn't say, either, that they were fit to eat. All resemblance to a real, Maine, wild blueberry was gratuitous. Some of my best roadside customers never came back, and some of my neighbors have been cool ever since. One man said he preferred his cranberries red, and another said he preferred cranberries anyway.

Since then I have done my seasonal blueberry gathering on the hills and barrens, just as I did before. I haven't blown a balloon since, and I find there was no need. The birds don't eat the things anyway, because there are no foolish birds. These tame and high-priced blueberries ripen behind my barn each year in profusion, enhance the vista beyond belief, and then fall to the ground with a hefty plunk I can hear up to a hundred yards. This is what happens to tame blueberries in a country where we can get the wild.

Then I thought, well, if this young woman from Boston doesn't know blueberries, maybe I can set her on my tame ones and they won't go to waste. She wouldn't know the difference.

And then I thought, well, that's kind of mean — after all, what did she ever do to me?

THE RATTLESNAKE KNIFE

Apropos of (and you can impone your bottom dollar that any essay is apropos of something) — now let's see, what was this about? Oh, yes — apropos of recent legislative enactments against knives, forbidding the populace to carry same because it is against the public safety (juvenile delinquency, you know), numerous comments have been made to me about knives, back when there was no delinquency. All agree that there was no threat to the body politic in the gleaming blade of olden time, and carrying

[35]

a knife had no side issue demanding the regulation of same.

It is important to note that the knife, now forbidden young people, was once a beautiful thing that belonged to growing up as a natural and unquestioned privilege. How we used to squat on the schoolyard grass (before hot-top was invented) and play "mumbly-peg" — a game that isn't in Hoyle. Some were good at nosies, but I never was. I shudder to think how we played with knives and nobody ever got stabbed.

One gentlemen stopped by and told how he possessed a famous and special knife, one he often drew from his pocket just to show people and brag. A knife that could well have gone to the Smithsonian Institution, and been framed to hang on the wall. One of those shake-the-hand-that-shook-the-hand-of-John-L.-Sullivan things. Not one shred of juvenile delinquency involved, and all legal. This knife, the man said, had actually cut the rattles off a rattlesnake!

You see, here in Maine we don't have rattlesnakes. We don't have any disagreeable reptiles. It's because of climate, geography, food, and good, clean politics. Maine is the only state that can say this, although Alaska and Hawaii may be able to as soon as they master a language. So, any rattlesnake lore around here is remarkable, and that's why this knife achieved distinction.

[36]

It was Topsham Fair time, an annual Sagadahoc County affair which comes in October, and like all little boys who live around here this gentleman had gone to the fair. He wasn't a gentleman then, you understand — just a boy with a knife. Topsham Fair hadn't grown up then, either, and it still had things to wonder you. Fairs now are all pari-mutuel excitement and not much for boys, and they don't have much to amaze you. The blasé quality of today's children distresses me — they don't get amazed at anything — and it was much better back when you could look at something and be surprised.

In those days Topsham Fair used to amaze you about every three feet. And a perennial amazement was a man who sold snake oil, which was good for man or beast. I would assume, in my elder times, that he came from some place like Belmont, Massachusetts, and that he was a fake, but in those days he said he came from Arizona and we believed him. He wore strange clothes, including funny boots with great high heels on them, and he spoke with outlander inflections, and he had little wire boxes full of rattlesnakes. As far as we knew, in those undelinquent days, the only place you might find a rattlesnake was either in Arizona or at the snake-oil pitch at Topsham Fair.

We boys found out that his routine was constant, and that he had a mercenary motive. He would twirl

[37]

a lasso and make believe he was roping a few cows, and he would shout as if a stampede had developed, and then when a few people gathered around to see what the noise was he would whip out a snake and make him rattle. In the brisk October weather of the State o' Maine the average rattlesnake is disposed to be languid, and it took a good deal of shaking and perseverance to get a fairish demonstration. But at this point a man in the crowd would suddenly appear to recognize the snake man and would say, "Well, Jim, you old cayuse you, how are you?" Jim would look up from his desultory snake and would appear to recognize the man and would cry out, "Why, Joe! How long you been out?"

This amused the circle of spectators, and the commercial aspects took over. Of course, the same man did this every time it was done, but this was obvious only to us boys — with the adults it authenticated everything and led smoothly into the sale of snake oil. They moved along; we stayed. So we didn't miss much. Jim would then give a stirring lecture on the thousandfold uses of snake oil and offer it to the great yearning populace at so much a bottle. The first few bottles would be eagerly snatched up by his confederates, after which the crowd would respond if it so desired. So things were.

Since it took quite a bit of doing for the man to get a decent rattle sometimes, as the sun crept behind the horse sheds in the afternoon he would move his act around to be in the sun. One of the rattlesnakes had, indeed, given up and was available for other purposes. During a lull in the sale of snake oil Jim donated this exotic asset to a couple of the local boys, and they spent the day running through the crowd astonishing everybody in all directions. One lady climbed right up the side of the exhibition hall.

It was a wonderful day and the two boys enjoyed every minute of it, but along in the afternoon the novelty wore off and the excitement subsided, so the boys decided they would remove the rattles from this unlucky creature and preserve them as a memento of a good time. They would also be an oddity in Maine. Now all the boys needed was a jackknife, and they didn't have one.

So my friend, who was recalling this, says he was standing idly by, watching something he has now forgotten, when these two young boys approached him and said, "Got a knife?" You don't just give your prized pocket knife to two boys and let them run off into a fair crowd, so this fellow went along with them. He didn't quite believe what they told him, anyway. So he saw what happened.

He says that knife thereupon took on a glory and magnificence beyond description. Word went all over the countryside that he had a knife which had cut the

[39]

rattles off a rattlesnake. People would ask him if he was the boy that had the knife. Other boys would ask to see it. "Which blade?" they would say.

He had numerous offers for his knife, any one of which would have catapulted him into opulence and prosperity. But nobody could entice him, and of course nobody could top him. Indeed, it now followed that he must at once procure another knife — one he could use, saving the famous one for exhibition only. He tells me he still has the knife, tucked away in a desk drawer, and although he is old and full of years he is still proud of it, and present-day legislation to outlaw knives makes him wonder.

FARMING AND "LARNING"

The assertion is now added that a young man, today, cannot expect to be a successful farmer, even, without a college education. This great news bursts upon us right in the era when a farmer can't afford to send his sons to college any more, and it looks like tough times ahead. How different from the old days when the farmer was the one member of society on whom an education was wasted! He didn't need to know anything. He was an unrecoverable hick, muddling along in his iggerant way just because he didn't have intelligence enough and knowledge enough to be anything else.

There have been a few farmers with college degrees, and I have known some of them. They were cultural-arts boys, as distinguished from the latter-day graduates of the cow-college, and this is important. One of these was a Harvard man, and I'm sure in those days Harvard had no courses in agronomy. Being a Harvard man in Maine is not quite the same as being one on State Street, and Jim didn't really look the role. Nobody around here tagged him as Ivy League. He was tall, lanky and gaunt, and in his bedraggled overalls looked not at all neo-Cantab. His diploma hung on the grainroom wall of his henhouse, festooned with spider webs and milling dust, and if you mentioned it Jim would say, "I went through Harvard to please my pa, and I took up poultry to please myself."

Jim would come to town with a wagon of crated eggs to put on the evening train, and to look at him you wouldn't think he knew beans. But there was a quiet dignity to his speech, and he had an aplomb the other farmers lacked. He never flaunted, but he was composed. One year, moved by his interest in affairs, he arose in Town Meeting and made a speech.

Town Meeting harangue is usually a homespun thing, spur of the moment and not in classical style. But Jim started a speech that came right out of Demosthenes and Cicero. Point by point it developed into an articulate unit of great art. He began long, involved sentences that held his listeners entranced and hung fire until he dropped in the key word; then he would shift to bright, staccato phrases that clipped the air off in sections. His voice rose or fell as some ancient Harvard professor of rhetoric had long since inculcated.

Arriving at the peroration, Jim summed things nicely, and reached the final athletic word with one hand held high, a single thin finger erected, and an appeal in his voice which would melt a stone. He sat down in a tumultuous silence, every man in the hall holding his mouth open in amazement. The effect was total. Education counts. Jim carried his vote without a dissenting murmur and the town talked about his speech for years. It was beautiful. That's how the town came to build a plank culvert on Middle Swamp Brook on the Maple Hill road.

Jim never played the character, but there was another educated farmer I knew who did. He didn't have his diploma hanging anywhere, lest somebody should see it. Once a year he would dress up and go to his college commencement, and he always looked like a minority senator calling at the White House. The rest of the time he lived in disreputable old farm clothes, and all summer he would go barefoot. Since he lived in an area with a lot of summer residents, he thought this was good for business, because he got a lot of free advertising as they told stories about him. One year he was gored badly by his bull. A monstrous great animal of mean disposition, the bull kept everybody frightened all the time, and nobody was surprised when the word ran around that Win had been second-best in a confrontation.

After Win got back in action, he used to sit around and tell of this adventure, hanging on all the details with relish and making all he could of it. One afternoon he had his bare feet up on the piazza rail, and he was telling a summer-lady how it happened. Properly appalled, she said, "Why Win, whatever did you do with the vicious beast!"

Win straightened up, struck a pose of magnificent satisfaction, and said with finality, "I et him!"

There was another farmer, much like Win, who frequently put his great knowledge to work and made out well. There was the time he "salvaged" a bus. This fellow lived on a back road, and when he roused about 3 A.M. at a churning noise across the way, he was astonished to see a big motor bus in his lane. Just then a knock came to his door, and it was the bus driver with an odd tale.

His bus had been chartered in Boston to deliver a load of Coast Guardsmen to the station at Rockland. He had made a wrong turn, and now in trying to reverse himself had got the bus mired in the pasture lane. Hub-deep in mud, the bus needed help. The driver asked the farmer if there was any chance of an extrication, whereat the farmer cranked up his heavy farm tractor and drove over in the dark to take a look. He attached a chain to the bus, drew the chain taut, then shut off the engine key and dismounted.

"Now," he said, "about my pay . . ."

The bus driver said the company would pay all right; there was no need to worry about that.

"I ain't worrying exactly," said this college-man farmer. "I just don't want to go through a lot of red tape and folderol to get my money. Suppose you pay me now."

The bus driver said he didn't have any money with him. "You better get some," said the farmer. "I don't budge 'til you do!"

The bus driver asked how much it would be, and the farmer said he figured it ought to be worth five dollars a ton. So the bus driver said he thought that was a little steep, and they'd better forget the whole thing. Said he'd telephone the Boston office and let them worry about it. "Just unhitch," he said. "I'll make other arrangements."

"Can't do that," said the educated farmer. "Laws of salvage. I got my line on her first. She's my prize."

"You old fool," said the bus driver. "This bus ain't no boat!"

So the farmer said, "Then why's she loaded with sailors?"

He stayed hitched and he got paid, and it goes to show what an education can do for agriculture.

OLYMPIC ICE HARVEST

When they held the winter Olympic Games at Squaw Valley, it was fun to sit in the comfort of the fireside without responsibility and watch the excitement on television. The temperature at Squaw Valley was reported as a brisk 40°, which we often attain here in Maine on a good summer day if the sun is out, and I was also disappointed in the speed attained in the slalom. Having been able, by determined restraint, to keep myself off skis all these years, I had a notion they whooshed right along, but when they put the time clock on the screen I noticed they were doing less than thirty miles an hour.

Some people can run faster than that, and I have two aged horses in the barn that can attain that speed on a hayrake. Thus I fell to wondering what we might have in Maine in the way of winter sports that would attract a crowd, and I decided the best show would be cutting ice. The way we used to do it at Weston's ice pond, anyway. When word went out that the ice had reached about fourteen inches, the winter sportsmen assembled, and they were a motley crew. The ice harvest was important to the town and was considered a community responsibility. Also, if the ice was now fourteen inches thick, a couple of healthy nights would stretch it to twenty-eight, and that was much too much. So everybody turned out. The Baptist minister would be working alongside a man who trained race horses, and the school superintendent would be helping the village ignoramus. The job was to get the house filled as fast as possible.

And there were no machines in the days I speak of. The ice was grooved by horses; end cakes were sawn by hand. The runway from the pond up to the saw-dust-insulated house had a steel frame that fitted over four cakes of ice, and the clevis on this frame was attached to a long rope that fed through pulleys to the horses up on the road. The frame had sharp teeth on the after end, to bite into the ice. When the four cakes were in place, the frame around them, and all in readiness, there would be a yell from the pond which the man up on the ramp would repeat. The horseman would then hear it, and he would drive. Up would go the cakes, all blue in the frigid light of a low January day, and the crew on the pond would get four more cakes in place.

There is no way to tell Squaw Valley Olympiacs how cold it used to be on an ice pond, but it was always closer to 40-below than 40-above. Putting in ice wasn't like chopping wood, where the exercise warms you. It was slow, bull-strength kind of work that brought no sweat. Everybody wore everything he could, and then he tied a binder twine around his middle — there is something about being tied in that holds body heat. The sun was never high enough to feel warm, and the wind had a way of finding you out there on the unsheltered ice.

Falling into the drink was standard practice. Even with creepers on, you'd thrust your weight against the hook-pole and your feet would flip, and as Porky Michaud put it, "I heard some splash an' I look, an' she was me!" This is the most awful ablution known to man. You'd go in and close the door behind you, and when you came up the man nearest would loop an ice hook into your mackinaw collar, jerk you back on the ice, and then you'd have the afternoon off. They didn't pay you for lost time, either. The longest trip you ever made in your life was from the water's brink to the shanty.

This shanty was a tar-paper shed to keep tools in

at night, and it doubled as a lunch room. The tin stove in it was kept aglow, and assuming that some-body would fall in, sooner or later, the foreman had wires overhead for drying clothes.

There was another way to get wet. Every once in a while the teeth on the steel hoisting frame would slip, and from away up on the runway four wild cakes of ice would slide back into the open water. If you were at a distance, it made a beautiful sight. The descent had all the grace — and more speed — of skiing. When the cakes hit the water the cascade was magnif-icent, and some of the water would freeze in the air before it came down to splash in the pond. But if you were not at a distance, and were occupied about the base of the runway, this was a hollow joy and you didn't just stand there and look at things.

The teamster would be the first to know the frame had slipped. His straining horses would lunge ahead as the weight was lost, and he would bellow, "Kout!" The man on the ramp would repeat it, and the men on the pond would run. If all went well, the monu-mental explosion when the four cakes hit the pond found everybody at a safe distance. If not, they all got soaked.

The day I fell in I was deftly jerked back onto the ice by Diddy Howland, and I went up to the shanty to put some sticks in the stove, undress, and hang my

wet clothes on the wires. Nobody went with me —
this was too routine. As soon as I got my clothes off
things seemed better, and shortly they were steaming
on the wires so the shanty was like a Finnish bath. I
sat there, looking at the woods through the one-pane
window, and listening to the muffled sounds of ice-
pond activity from the other direction. Voices, the
creaking of ropes, the metallic click of the frame as
it came and went — all these sounds were muted by the
intense cold, and I sat naked, warm and cozy, waiting
for my clothes to dry. Then came the tumult.

I heard the wild shouts from the teamster, the echo
from the top of the runway. I heard the *whooomph*
as the blocks of ice rammed into the pond water. Then
silence, and I supposed all was well. But almost at once
the door of the shanty opened and in came three dripping ice-cutters — they had fallen in their rout and
had taken the full splash flat on their faces on the ice.

In they came, and they stripped, and I helped them
hang their clothes up in the wires. That afternoon, in
the steam, we four sat on wooden boxes, warm and
unclothed, and we had the greatest cribbage game in
the annals of winter sports. You should have seen it.
Squaw Valley, indeed.

YAMS AND YACHTS

It has been my whimsy, ever since the computing machine appeared, to punch little holes in any card I get. The little cards all say, "Do not fold, spindle or mutilate," but they have holes in them and I can't see how one or two more holes would make much difference. I didn't really know much about computer machines, and I was just bent on idle amusement, but now that I have found out about them I intend to make this a life work.

Every so often you hear somebody make cozy remarks about the old country store. Everybody deplores the trend away from it. People liked molasses barrels. I'm sure customers of the modern chain grocery don't realize how complete this trend has become, and when I heard that one of our wholesale grocers had installed a big computer machine I took the time to go and look. The identical same relentless inventions that track the pioneering orbits of space are now handling the corn flakes.

It's a terrible thing to contemplate; and I speak as one who has gone and contemplated. I've seen it.

This machine is not a simple little office model, but is a big, vast, complete unit that occupies its own air-conditioned apartment and requires trained operators in whom the company has made a substantial investment. It is the same machine SAC uses to scan the skies in defense. But it was acquired and retained solely to do the bookkeeping for a wholesale grocer. One may, upon hearing anything like this, say uh-huh, but when they told me the president of the firm had used the machine to predict the outcome of the Monhegan Island yacht race, I hurried right over.

Part of this outrageous story hinges on the fact that the machine is bigger than the company needs. They hope to grow, but even so the capacity of the computer will never be taxed. The machine does the payrolls, figures all taxes and fringes, keeps warehouse inventories, schedules a fleet of trucks and keeps their mileage, fluctuates prices as the market varies, does all billing, enters receipts and discounts — in short does everything in connection with running the largest food-handling business in Maine. Yet they use only two per cent of the machine.

Just a short time ago a big regional business survey was made in that area, and the crew that did it was out about six months. They brought together every known fact, from the temperature of harbor water back to the flora in the suburbs. Then they came to this grocery company and asked if they might "store" all this information in the machine. They used the other end of the thing, so the female help potential wouldn't get mixed up with the price of prunes, and they fed it all in and went away. Meantime the grocery business went along as usual. After quite a few months this survey company returned, and when they pressed a button the machine began writing them a book. The profit on canned peaches had declined about two cents in the meantime, but it didn't show up in the population densities or the home-ownership ratio in the Woodfords section.

This kind of thing worries me a great deal, although I can't say why, and when I heard about the Monhegan Island yacht race I felt I should inform myself. The president of the grocery firm is a friend of mine, although a yachtsman himself, and teased by the intricate possibilities of the machine he had just purchased, he got the idea of foretelling the outcome of the annual regatta. The race is the big event of the Portland Yacht Club each year, and draws entries from all up the coast. It is a handicap race, where elapsed time is not critical. A machine would have to be good. So the grocer made himself a project of this, and went to work.

He fed in the physical measurements of each boat — beam, length, waterline, mast height, and all. He fed in the age, weight, length, political affiliation and waist measurement of each skipper. He added the schooling, nautical experience, etc., arriving at a maritime intelligence quotient for each. He took the long-range weather average, applied it mathematically to each vessel, and superimposed the mean tide run, give or take average wind velocities times distance.

What appealed to him was that the methods now being pursued were exactly the methods used on yams and avocados, butt hams and ready-to-brown rolls. While he was busy playing at his end of the machine, the other end was running the business, and they never misplaced a potato chip. And when he thought he had all the pertinent information properly adjusted and entered, and he had rechecked the entries, he pressed the master switch and stood back.

The machine gave a hump, wheels turned, sparks flew, and the front lit up like Times Square. Then the keyboard flew into a frenzy, and the little tape started to run out of the slot. One after another the names of the yachts appeared, all arranged in order, elapsed time adjusted to the handicap, and the race was over.

With much interest, you may be sure, this grocer attended the Monhegan Race that week end. Tape in hand, he watched the progress, and at the finish line he watched the yachts come in exactly as his machine had placed them. The same infallible accuracy that dispatches prunes to South Berwick and soap powder to Milford had unerringly predicted the outcome of the yacht race! The frightening moral being, of course, that henceforth there is no sound reason for ever holding the Monhegan Race. Just give the list of entries to your grocer!

The larger moral, however, is even more so. There is no longer any reason for having a grocer at all. A trained operator at a machine, in a distant place, can run hundreds of identical stores all over the region. People with memories of pressing their noses against a glass, pointing at licorice sticks and saying, "And one of those . . ." while the friendly grocer patiently waited for childhood minds to be made up — we can only shudder at this. This machine not only fills orders and dispatches them, but it tells the retailer how much money he'll make when he sells the goods! I saw it and I know. That's why I always punch little holes in any card I get that says, "Do not mutilate."

UNCLE ELIJAH'S SELF-DEFENSE

Something was said in the living room the other evening about the importance of national defense, and the way it came out I thought about Uncle Elijah's goad-stick. This was a smooth maple wand, neither rigid nor supple — "souple," as he said it — with the handle end well worn from long years of holding in his calloused hand, and it was used for teaming the oxen. Now, on the far end, the one next to the oxen, there was a brass ferrule which was really a .45-70 rifle shell, and bedded in the end-grain was a needle. It was a household sewing needle, right out of Aunt Affia's kit, and it would pierce tough homespun cloth readily enough and no doubt would pierce the tough hide of an ox.

The difference being that Uncle Lije never bradded an ox in his life, and would as soon have beaten up his devoted wife. The point on the end of the ox-goad was the only tool on the whole farm that never got used — and I mean, at all. Indeed, because he loved his wife, Uncle Lije loved his oxen even more. He spent more time with them, anyway, and he would as soon have taken the goad-stick to her as to them. He was a soft-hearted man, and the brad on his goad-stick was superfluous.

The word goad, incidentally, shouldn't be confused with gored. Maine-isms do require special understanding, and goad-stick may sound to some as repetitive. It was a stick, and it was a goad. The same with hand-scythe — if you just say scythe you get all there is. Probably hound-dog is another example. I never heard anybody say goad; it was always goad-stick. As for gored, we had a saying that it makes a difference whose ox is being gored. It's fun when it happens to another fellow, but you don't laugh so hard when it happens to you. Since oxen are placid and not given to goring, the expression loses some sense if you analyze, and my whole reason for going into this is my belief, as a child, that Uncle Elijah's goad-stick was used for goring. Every teamster did have a brad in his goad-stick, and some of them used them. I make it clear, however, that the needle in Uncle Lije's stick was longer, sharper and shinier than the common run of goads. When you used one, you had a dull brad that poked rather than penetrated. Uncle Elijah's was wholly for show.

Nowadays, if you want the ultimate, you can buy a patented ox-goad that has little dry cells in the handle, and when you press the end against the flank of a steer an electric shock does what the brad used to. It is low-voltage, and so is the disposition of an ox, and they say this is more humane. Since the whole idea is to get an animal into gear, I doubt if the mentality of a steer will see that much difference.

Uncle Elijah's cattle were close to him. They were fat, tenderly cared for. They walked beside him, as he walked beside them, man partner to the beast. They were powerful animals who started walking beside him when they were little, and they knew how to respond to the bending of his knee — just as they did to soft clucks in his teeth and whoa-heishes. He had them so well trained that when he turned them loose in the pasture they would feed with their heads down together, side by side, as if they were still under the yoke. Always nigh and off.

They were handsome, sleek, and always beautifully groomed. If Uncle Lije was obliged to put them through mud, he'd spend hours afterward washing them down clean. He would pass a hand down a flank with such an expression of pleasure that you wouldn't believe. They were a power plant that had no being, actually, apart from his. If he stopped them to rest a moment, the nigh ox would lean against him as he stood there, settling over slowly with affection. When he teamed them this goad-stick with its rapier-like needle would be held in his left hand, away from the animals, just the opposite of what other teamsters did.

Then he would throw his right arm over the shoulder of the nigh animal, and by leaning ahead he would convey that they were to begin. You'd see them strain slowly into the yoke and bows, and when the slack came taut you'd hear him whisper, "Now!" and all three of them would strain ahead and move the biggest boulder in the field.

Most farmers did it quite otherwise. They would dance around and yell, wave the stick and bring it down on flanks. They would make a performance out of teaming. You can still see that kind of ox driver at the county fairs, where they make quite an attraction and people pay to get in.

Not Uncle Lije. He never had to put on a show. When his calves were first able to stand he went to work with them. He petted them along. A whisper, a hand around an ear, a sucking through a tooth — he brought them along so they thought as he did, and he as they, until no gymnastics were needed. He always carried his goad-stick, of course. It was the badge of a teamster, and anybody walking beside oxen had to have a goad-stick.

Even though he never used it, the brad in Uncle Lije's goad-stick was three times as long as that of anybody else. It was honed to a point, and oiled. When the sun struck it there would be a flashing. To those who held that a goad-stick should merely capture the attention of a beast, not impale him, this was a tremendous goad-stick. And, of course, every once in a while somebody would ask why, with such meticulously trained beasts, Uncle Elijah had to carry such an exceptional goad-stick. It was a good question. Uncle Lije had a good answer. "Self-defense," he would say, chuckling away to himself at the very notion that his darling oxen would ever attack.

IT'S THAT TIME AGAIN!

The non sequitur is the commonest indication that the season has advanced and spring housecleaning is on the make. The first one or two slip over my head, but about the third one I rally to the warning and take heed. I usually move my fishing rod out to the shed, so it will be handy if I want to sneak away. I'm not a coward — I'm just that smart. This time the tip-off was a clear one, and I caught the following right on the button:

(At breakfast)

SHE: Is that egg done enough?

ME: Fine, fine.

SHE: Do you want more toast?

ME: Great plenty, thanks.

SHE: Do you know where Millie got the pegs?

In the spring of the year any alert husband will recognize this as an open warning. Eating his egg, he will pause with the spoon halfway to his mouth and will have one of those unreal, vacant, blank spasms of mental hiatus in which he has no idea how Millie got in, who she is, what pegs are and why this is going on at all. But he will realize that housecleaning time has come again. Now begins the business of airing winter blankets on the line and laying them away for fall. Everything is tipped up, turned over and pushed aside. Rising from breakfast the intelligent husband will go into his den, find his rod and reel, set them in the shed, and govern himself accordingly. Still, who is Millie? What pegs?

Millie? Well, about ten years ago she was driving past on the road and she saw our stub-tailed cat on the lawn and as she always wanted a stub-tailed cat she came in to see if we'd sell. Or did we know where she could find another? And as she stood in the kitchen door talking cats she could see Mel Thompson and me at the table settling the world's champeenship cribbage title. It was two out of three, and I skunked him one. Millie, who was unknown to us until then, remarked that she'd rather play cribbage than eat, so I beat her two games and then she went away.

But a week or so later, pleased because we had told her where to get a cat, she brought in a little wooden box with a lid, and in it were six little hand-carved ivory cribbage pegs. She thought it was a shame to be using common kitchen matches to keep score on a walnut cribbage board. Thank you, she said, and we never saw her again.

But, you see, housecleaning time was now at hand;

the tree swallows were back and the lilac buds were swelling; and that morning she thought she would start with the living room. No man would ever guess just where she will start. It's like building a house on the prairie. How did the old settlers decide, on perfectly flat land, just where they would put a house? Why not twenty feet to the west, or fifty feet to the east? What difference did it make? A great American conundrum. What difference does it make where you start cleaning house? But this time she began with the handsome antique cobbler's bench I had made that winter, and my cribbage board happened to be on it. Somebody else and I had just settled the world's champeenship again, and we left the board handy. So as she grabbed the cobbler's bench and whirled it around, the cribbage board slid off and one of the pegs rolled across the floor and she couldn't find it. She hunted, but it eluded her. Gone. So if she knew where Millie got those pegs, she could replace it, perhaps. I got my fishing things out, and stretched a line between the house and the shed for blankets, and it is now the time.

Man, as distinguished from woman, plays no real part in this vernal exercise. There is nothing about the up-in-a-heaval that he can fathom intellectually. There is nothing about the work, really, that he can do. She knows which chairs get moved that way and which this, but no mental equipment has been vouch-safed to man to let him understand it. He has a good head for some things, and his back will boost about as well as anybody's, but the telltale non sequitur of breakfast indicates more is coming and he can't grasp any of it. If he tries to help, or is forced to help, he becomes dismayed and befuddled by the unrelated inconsistencies, and if he doesn't soon start a fight he goes fishing.

Going fishing is better. The far place, because you have to hang around to make a good fight amount to anything. Besides, I'm a veteran at this now, and re-alize my judgment is better than my courage. Too many times, when I was younger and inclined to be congenial, I would try to be helpful and it just doesn't work. Too many times I have heard her say, "Why can't we put that towel rack here, instead of there?"

There is an excellent reason why we cannot; it has to do with original construction of the premises and the architectural fact that studs are set 16 inches on center. The towel rack goes into a stud there, and it would not have a stud over here. "Why can't we move the stovepipe around the other way?" she asks. The main reason is that it has to go into a chimney, which I find is not easy to explain to a housecleaning woman. Then she will point at a three-hundred-and-fifty-pound bureau and say, "Lift that while I plug in the lamp!" When she said that I looked at her lovingly and I said, "You lift it, and I'll plug," and then I went fishing.

In spite of the fact that I have disproved it many times, she still thinks housecleaning would be easier if I helped. Easier for her, not easier for me. The thing is not physical, really. I can move a sofa, but I never could understand why it has to be lifted over a bed. I can move a sofa, but I never know where or why. When I come home she looks at me as if she is tired and it's my fault. I never really feel as if I shirked. Not really.

Because the female omits to assess the most important point of all. That a man is so vastly inferior at this time that it engulfs him quite. He is mentally unhappy at getting involved in something beyond his ability. He is just eating an egg, when ivory cribbage pegs thrust him into confusion. Deep down, he knows this is lucid, logical, and sound as a nut. But it's a woman's nut, and he can't cope with it. He's licked. I got three trout, one of them over ten inches.

WOODLAND CHILD'S PLAY

All the analysts and experts are wrong and I can tell you what has happened to the United

States of America without any surveys and studies, and it will take just a few words — children don't play in the woods any more. Great lamentation is made on every hand about juvenile delinquency and the lack of purpose in the beat generation, and all the answer anybody needs is to walk up through a woodlot and see that there are no children there. There used to be children there, back before things disintegrated, and they'd have quite a program going that, as far as I know, never attracted the attention of specialists and sociologists.

It wasn't just the play, although that alone was magnificent and unlimited. It was the imagination that went with it, the opportunity to be so many things, in so many ways, and the variety of objects that were strewn around to become aware of and sentient about. So much was available, and so much to tease the wonder!

My own woods happened to be properly situated for maximum use. And I say "my own" not so much because the warranty deed defines them by rod and chain, but because I grew up in them long before any material possession accrued. They were one and the same with the mysterious region Lewis and Clark explored; they were Sherwood Forest; they could be the scene of a Stanley and Livingstone, or of Groseilliers and Radisson. It was all one.

The old range roads of Maine broke the farm country up in units of approximately a mile. They wandered as hills and brooks suggested, so there was nothing checkerboardish. Our farmhouse was on the far side of a range, and the village was on the other. This meant that our woods were closer to the town than our house was, and thus they invited children from downtown, and they came to play with us farm boys. Today, long after village boys have stopped playing in my woods, the situation remains the same — our house is out in the country, but our woodlot runs to the town.

It's forlorn to walk up through those woods today, and think of the magnificent opportunities the village boys are missing. Country boys, too, for that matter. There's nobody there. I can look up in pines and see wonderful places to make tree houses, and nobody has a tree house. Some of our tree houses were just limbs with imaginary boards, but we'd sit there and enjoy them.

My own youngsters are grown up, so I have no rapport now to know what the younger folks are doing instead of playing in my woods. Whatever it is, it's occupying the public concern, and it isn't swinging on birches. A whole new stand of paper birches has come in along the edge of the maple grove, and they

[65]

are going to waste — not a child has yet swung on them!

There are no limbs on a smooth birch of this kind and size, for hands and feet, and to get up into one you must "shinny." It's like climbing a pole. And after you get up far enough the tree will bend under your weight and it will swing you out and down until you land on the ground again light as a pussy cat. Then the tree straightens up, and you can climb it again. Unless there is a misfire.

That's when you don't shinny fast enough and don't get up far enough, and the tree begins to bend before your weight is in the right place. This leaves you far out, but not down. About fifteen feet off the ground, maybe, and no place to go. If you'd gone a mite higher the tree would have bent all the way — or if you'd weighed a bit more. There you are, hollering away, and everybody finds it amusing. You have a kind of summit decision to make, and no matter how you ponder things there is really only one outcome — you let go. This was never so bad as you expected, and next time you scramble much harder to get your weight up higher. I wonder just what special lessons were taught by swinging birches that a mechanical exerciser in a city park can't teach?

We used to have meeting places. After a day of play we'd break up to go home, agreeing to meet next time at "Number One." This was under a monstrous red oak amongst the lower pines. It stuck up so high the pine limbs crowded in under it, and as you looked up you thought you saw a big oak tree with pine needles on it. That was Number One. When we built our new house I put the saw to Number One, and that's where we got the red oak planks in our living room. It's still Meeting Place Number One.

Meeting Place Number Two was a ledge above the spring, a safe place to have a fire. When we took lunches, that was the place. Most always, if we were Englishmen we'd meet at Number One, but Indians met at Number Two. It was a better place to dry scalps.

There were no cowboys then, just Englishmen and Indians. The Englishmen always lost if we had a fight, and got scalped. We were hard on Englishmen, except that sometimes the Indians were at peace, and would be very kind to the Englishmen and teach them many things.

But there was so very much more. We trudged through deep snow and had winter picnics, but when we found the skunk cabbages coming through the ice in the swamp we knew the long summer lay ahead with really good times. Soon somebody would find a hepatica, and then a Stinking Benjamin (which was wonderful for bouquets for school if you had a green teacher!) and one day a moccasin flower. We had a rule, I don't remember how it came about, that May-flowers and moccasin flowers were never picked. Somehow we knew that gathering them harms the roots and they often fail to come again, so we left them.

We found partridge and woodcock nests, and we'd climb great pines to bring down a baby crow for a pet. Every boy had a pet crow, one time or another, and you didn't have to keep him in a cage. If you worked with him enough you could get him to say hello. It sounded more like "haw-haw," but it was hello, all right. Some of the old-timers used to tell us if you split a crow's tongue you could get him to talk even better than a parrot. But we knew that was a joke. You get to know things like that by climbing a pine for a crow and then looking at his tongue. Things like that are worth knowing.

One of the nicest things about playing in the woods was coming home at night. We'd have something to eat around the spring at Number Two, and listen to the woods settling in for dusk. We'd call crows and watch them fly over the trees, trying to figure out what the noise was about. And then we'd head for home. The village boys would go down the woodroad into the pines, and I'd come up over the hill towards the farmhouse. I'd come out of the junipers to see the lamplight in the windows down across the fields. Always careful to avoid ambushes, and wary of snapping a twig to betray my presence, I'd scout the situation and find the settlement safe. It was good to know that while you were supporting the pioneer hardships, the loved ones were cozy and comfy. Little did they know the dangers that prevailed, and the security assured them by your stealthy watch.

This and much, much more. Every time I wander up through my woods nowadays, it grieves me that there is no evidence of child's play. The forest is there as it always was — friendly, informative, inviting. But nobody makes a lean-to, there are no houses in the trees, and there are no ashes at Number Two. Nobody has tracked an Englishman, nor have the Pemaquids dried any scalps. Yet the foundations grant funds for surveys and Youth is a national problem. I think it's a terrible thing we've come to.

CHARLEY AND THE AFRICAN VIOLETS

The producers of the "Antique Show" on Educational Television may be disturbed to learn that we laugh at it, because they don't know it's funny. We think it's one of the funniest shows to watch. The other evening a man held up a chair and asked the lady on the panel to discuss it, and she began by saying, "Yes, this is a chair." We could see it was a chair, and we could also see that it is just like one we have up in the barn chamber with a rich and long history that includes the time Father tripped over it in the dark and rammed his head into Mother's bench of African violets. The noisy subsequence indicated that Mother thought more of her violets than she did Dad, and it was difficult afterwards to convince Dad he had any love for the chair. I put the chair up in the barn some years since, and I doubt if I bring it down even though we learned the other night on ETV that it will fetch a pretty penny. It has values I wouldn't care to sell.

I forgot to state that Charley, our ancient tomcat, was asleep on the chair when Father tripped over it. Charley, from long experience, didn't trust people, and anybody who disturbed him overmuch was likely to hear about it.

One of Charley's best reasons for mistrust was Grammie Gundersen, who was a dear lady with a heart of gold who came to live with us once in one of those neighborhood arrangements now quite lost in the bygone. I think she had money, but money isn't always a true test of need, and after things sort of folded up for her she had "no place to go." We always called her Grammie Gundersen, although she was no grammie to us. She never paid a cent for the years she stayed happily at our house; we didn't ask and she didn't offer. She had no lawful claim on our hospitality, and any suggestion of charity was dispelled because she "took a-holt" and did heroic work in running our home.

Grammie Gundersen was a huge woman, and any trace of femininity which she may have had was either gone or hidden. She had feet like baker's peels and she handled them athwart, like a side-wheel ferry boat. She wore high boots of the lumberman's kind, with rawhide lacings looped through the hook eyelets. And she did everything at top speed. She'd lope through the house like a horse, indifferent to everything except her momentary purpose, and Father, Mother, children, guests — and finally Charley — found it was smart to keep out of her way and let her go it.

So on one particular morning, in the winter, Grammie Gunderson arose in her back upper chamber and came down the front stairs and out into the kitchen to start the porridge. It was still dark — she would light a lamp, touch off the stove, and thus arrange to have the day proceed.

At that time Charley was a fairly new cat and as the night wore along he would go in and sleep on the hot air register in the front room. During the night our wood-burning furnace would dwindle, until by morning only a faint sniff of heat was coming up. Charley never had any problem about sleeping, so sometimes we'd go down in the morning and fire up the furnace and he'd keep right on sleeping over the register until he began to fry. Then he would wake, glance around to see if anybody noticed how foolish he looked, and move over to a cool place and go back to sleep.

And this morning when Grammie Gundersen descended she rounded the doorway from the front hall and caught the sleeping Charley with one of her great, gorming, flat boots, and she mowed a swath with him right out through into the kitchen. Every time Charley came down she would cuff him again, and as she moved along he moved right along with her. He finally landed with a splat against the kitchen wall and was safe when she veered off and groped in the dark for a match by the lamp shelf. Charley staggered to his feet with appropriate comments.

The family, all still in bed, had been awakened by this. The general sound suggested a torture chamber of the Inquisition, where somebody was beating people to a pulp, and when Charley hit the wall we all found out what caterwauling means. Grammie Gundersen was the only person who didn't know anything about this — she was a little hard of hearing anyway, but with the porridge on her mind she had no place for Charley.

Long after Grammie Gundersen left us to go and live with a grandson who finally got married, the merest mention of her name in family conversations would bring Charley up from a deep sleep and send him to the door yowling for out, and any disturbance in the home such as dropping a plate or slamming a closet door would terrify him. Consequently, in his old age, when Father tripped over the antique chair it sent Charley into a frenzy of panic, and he was taking the house down in all directions while Father was picking the African violets from his ear.

And Uncle Roscoe, who liked to retire early and read Zane Grey in bed, was riding the purple sage at the time, and when he heard Father and Charley he sat right up in bed and shouted "Grammie Gundersen's back!" That's what Charley thought.

So, you see, we find much hilarity in the antique show on ETV. It isn't what they do and say, it's what we add to it from our own affairs. When the lady said, "Yes, this is a chair," she didn't know about Grammie Gundersen. When they tell us the chair is extremely valuable we know they are not computing any Charleys and any African violets.

AFTER-SCHOOL JOBS

It's barely possible I am about to expound some great truths. I got to thinking about it while watering pansies the other morning. I don't like to sell too many pansies, because every time you sell one you sell a trowel of the farm with it. But they do bring in a springtime penny, so I basket some up and put them by the roadside to catch tourists. And I have to go out once or twice a day and give them a drink, and as I was doing this I said to myself, "What am I watering pansies for? That's a boy's job!"

But, of course, there was no boy. I wouldn't know where to apply to restore ancient affairs when a youngster came around looking for something to do. The day is gone, the thing is past — yet perhaps we'd better find him before we collapse altogether.

It's not at all an economic thing; it's a matter of continuation of the arts. Pupils stood by the great painters of the Renaissance, but nobody stands by me to see how to water pansies. How is anybody going to water pansies unless somebody shows him? And who is there to show? Not that I want to start heavy argument about minimum wages and social betterment, although I guess I could. The general trend has been to discourage and forbid the growing boy the advantages of after-school jobs, and today almost all the things he ought to be doing are illegal. Public attitudes dissuade. And, of course (as with most human things you legislate), it isn't working out just as they said it would.

Does anybody think I'm going to pay a boy a dollar twenty-five an hour to water pansies? Even if he wanted to? So, you see, they haven't legislated wages at all; they've merely put pansy-watering out of business and deprived some boy of the wonderful chance to be associated with me. Not just companionship, which I have in excellent measure; but the opportunity to learn the things that can only be learned at the side of a Renaissance painter, or a man who has odd jobs to do.

The big word is "exploiting." The new system is intended to prevent folks like me from exploiting the boy. Fair labor practices. The main trouble with this notion is that back in the days of blissful ignorance we boys didn't know we were being exploited. As I recall all the after-school jobs I had, every one of them a rich lesson in vocational training and the humanities, and every one of them exploiting me shamefully, I can see now that this exploitation was very valuable to me.

I mowed lawns and shoveled snow, of course, but

there were countless other opportunities. First of all, and it is no longer so, we would go looking for jobs. We'd go to a door and knock, or we'd walk out into the field and ask the farmer. I got a fine job that way with Miss Foster, maiden daughter of a long line of ships' captains, and she had nothing to do but live on the family fortunes and keep the big white house pretty. She said she'd give me a try, and afterwards she said I was a good worker. It was wonderful to share the responsibilities of keeping up the old Foster place.

In the fall I helped her tip down the rosebushes, and then all winter I looked forward to bringing them out again in the spring. Carrying a silk parasol, Miss Foster showed me how to prune them, and I have always been one of the best rosebush pruners in town—Foster Method. She wasn't a bit backward about finding fault if I did something the wrong way, but she always took that next step and showed me the right way.

By all standards, Miss Foster was above reproach. There was never the slightest thought in all the town that she would "exploit" a small boy. True, she would fish all around in her purse trying hard to find a coin that was worth more than five cents, and would apologize much if she couldn't. Sometimes by rare luck she would find a dime. And she always accom-

[76]

panied payment with a friendly preachment on the importance of being faithful and reliable, and the virtues of thrift.

And wouldn't you just have a time of it today trying to explain to a Commissioner of Labor and Industry what a fine thing it was to get a job in a blacksmith shop! We used to race for that one, because Boomer Dunphy, the smith, made a practice of hiring the first boy who arrived after school. Some days he'd have a stack of new iron to lay in the racks and rods to fit under the bench. Maybe stock shoes to size on the wall pins. At least the place always needed sweeping up. It was wonderful to feel you were part of that business, and when you were working around and somebody brought in a green western horse to get a shoe tightened, there was little more in life to look forward to. There was always a fight with green western horses, and I loved to be "exploited" while I held the beast's nose into the rafters on a "twister." We always got 'em shod!

If the blacksmith exploited us in hours and wages, and put us in situations the safety-committee deplores, he overpaid us in the excitement and lore that went along with it. A blacksmith shop was a place where the boy could work for nothing, and be well paid. How else would you get a beautiful finger ring made from a horseshoe nail? I never felt the least bit exploited, even when the blacksmith said business was slow and after I had swept and boosted he could find only a few coppers in his pocket.

We cleaned out cellars and sheds, stacked firewood, washed stormsash and put on screens, picked berries, and ran millions of errands. One year I got a chance to paint blinds on the Marsden Mansion — doing them one at a time across two apple barrels. On rainy days the painters would help, but I did the rest by myself. I got ten cents an hour for that job, but I also got instructions from the best boss house-painter in town. If I was used, I also learned to paint.

And this was always true. We learned always how to do things. We were willing, and so was our instructor. Our skills increased and widened. We learned the importance of doing as we were told, the importance of the tricks to every trade. There are tricks, even, in watering pansies. We learned what tools were for, and how to use them. And, when all is said, I think the money we got was worth something, too. The nickels and dimes we laid by were not easily come by, but we got them. And I valued them the day I bought me a bicycle. Tell me, how does a boy earn a bicycle nowadays?

ROSES AND FAMILY ROOTS

Every year we put some roses on the hoewood table, for thus Aunt Eunice came to know Aunt Helen. We are great on aunts, although we aren't too much a family-tree family — I mean, I can tell you all about aunts, but I'm not always sure just where they came in the plan. Genealogists will give you dates and parentage. And neither Aunt Eunice nor Aunt Helen has ever descended to a statistic in our house. They hang around. That's what the bowl of roses on the hoewood table is all about.

Aunt Eunice was mine. Aunt Helen was not. Aunt Eunice lived with the family away back in the beginning, and since she had nowhere else to live she made herself useful in ten thousand ways. The pioneer household had plenty for her to do, from fitting firewood to minding babies, but she remained a maiden aunt and did not communicate onward via progeny. But she did plant roses by the front door, and a perennial and everlasting routine was started when somebody first said, "Mind Aunt Eunice's roses!" Somebody was always careless and somebody was always mindful. They were the red roses of the House of Lancaster, and Aunt Eunice had brought the roots from England to see if the strange climate of a foreign field would nourish them. It did; it does — they still grow by our front door, and every June-time enough get cut to fill a silver bowl on the hoe-wood table of Aunt Helen.

The wonderful thing about Aunt Eunice's roses is that they thrive in neglect. Other kinds of roses need attention, and bugs and blights bother them. But Aunt Eunice's go along year after year and we never do anything with them or for them. Their little buds burst, fill the dooryard with fragrance, and then the petals shed by next morning. So Aunt Eunice comes a-visiting each year, and back at the old stand is well remembered by generations who never laid eyes on her.

I have imagined her as a prim English spinster who had no great love for pioneering, but who felt family-bound to come here and see that her brothers made out. The hardships probably distressed her, but duty was above her own preferences. The brother who came here and cleared a farm gave her bed and board, and she repaid him many times over. I hope the wandering savages who visited our dooryard in those times leaned over to sniff her roses — Aunt Eunice would certainly have appreciated this approval of the little bit of home she had transplanted to New England. Lancaster roses and the pines of Maine!

But Aunt Helen is quite another matter. She belongs to Will and Lillian Harding, who are friends, and in her own time Aunt Helen went wandering too. She went to Yokohama after Japan was "opened," and she was the office force in that city for Wells-Fargo. If you think Wells-Fargo was a stagecoach and a man with a horse on Channel 10 every Tuesday night, you are unaware of Aunt Helen, who tossed her curls in adieu at her home state of Maine and shipped to the inscrutable East to seek her fortune. Maine people had been about everywhere by that time, in their home-built vessels, and the sudden opening of Japan offered them a new place to trade. Aunt Helen was among the first to embrace this opportunity. And she was a sharp woman who looked out for Number One. The vessels that plied between Japan and home brought many a souvenir of her astuteness. She managed things very well for Wells-Fargo, but whenever she saw a chance to dabble she didn't let her loyalties to the company interfere with free enterprise. She invested privately, too. And as the years rolled by her family back in Maine accumulated boxes, bundles and bales of Aunt Helen's freight, holding it for instruction or for Aunt Helen's return in retirement.

At one time she sent home a shipload of hoewood tables, curiously and cunningly made. The Japanese craftsmen turned them out in six pieces — four legs, a lower shelf and a top — and they fitted together without glue or fastenings. Once the parts were fitted together they would not come apart — the joints were perfectly made. The top, three feet square, was exquisitely hand carved in an Oriental pattern. The investment in these tables in Japan had been small, but they would certainly fetch a fine figure in this country, and it is odd that they never got sold, but have remained ever since in Will Harding's barn attic.

The reason is that the parts got mixed up somewhat. Will found that you couldn't just take four legs, a shelf and a top, and make a table. You had to find the precise six pieces originally meant for each particular table, and a part of one table wouldn't fit into the hole of another. Extending six to the Nth power gives you the variables of Aunt Helen's chances, and the hazards of doing business in Japan.

Aunt Helen never came home. And Will Harding, who inherited her Oriental treasures, used to go up in the barn attic once in a while and play with the table pieces like a puzzle. He would hunt until he found a leg that would go into a top, shout, "Eureka!" and then hunt for another leg that would go into the same top. Once, long ago, Will promised me that the next one he fitted together should be mine, and years later he came bringing it. He chugged into the door-yard in the time of Aunt Eunice's roses, and he lifted the parts of the hoewood table from the back seat of his Stanley Steamer and showed me how they all went together and would never come apart again.

Thus Aunt Helen became something to us, and her table is so out-of-place in our Early Yankee living room that everybody notices it and asks wherever did we get it? Then we tell about Aunt Helen, and she gets remembered, too, and once a year we put Aunt Eunice's roses on Aunt Helen's table. This is known as "having roots," which more and more people now-adays are not having. Right?

NOSE TO THE GRINDSTONE

"No," said Jimmie Griffin the other day. "We don't touch a hand-scythe at all no more nowadays. Haying has changed."

"Then I don't suppose you'd want to buy a good grindstone?" asked my friend Flats Jackson, in the tone of voice he likes to adopt when he assumes a philanthropic role, and hopes to stick some innocent bystander with a rough trade. Jimmie said he guessed not.

"That's too bad," said Flats. "I got the best grind-stone anybody ever had, and it's legally mine, and it's available at a young and tender price."

"I suppose it's a coarse stone," I said.

"No, it's not," said Flats. "It's coarser than medium, but it don't draw on the metal too bad, and it's a quick cutter without being flinty, if you know what I mean."

"How did you ever come to own a grindstone *legally?*" I asked.

"I bought it. I bought it from old man Guppy up above Fairbanks."

Nobody said anything, so Flats said, "The mean Guppy."

Nobody said anything again, so Flats went on, "I suppose this Guppy was the meanest man that ever set foot on the State of Maine. He had an ingrown belief that nobody under fifteen should ever have any fun at all, and that over fifteen you had outlived the desire for it. I can't tell you all the mean things that man did. But we boys around there used to like to work on his disposition when we could think of anything, and sometimes the more agile-minded were able to contrive a situation that should have reformed him. I reformed him, once.

"Well, on the night before the Fourth I took it into my head to give him an opportunity, and I took it out on his grindstone. It took a lot of doing, because a grindstone is heavy and I was walking a lot closer to the ground then. But I wanted this to be a big surprise, and the harder it was to do the better it would turn out.

"Today, naturally, I don't have any idea why this was supposed to be funny or nice, or why it was supposed to reform old man Guppy, or why I elected to work so hard on such a small possibility. But I stole up behind his barn and went into the shed, and with the strength of ten men I lifted that great gorming grindstone down out of the stand and got it on the ground.

"It was a hand-crank stone. The kind that set on four rollers, and the shaft came out with two bends in it for cranking. Funny no old Yankee ever figured out a way to put a clutch on a grindstone. When you got one like this rolling, and the bearings were free, she'd larrup along for a half hour after you got done turning, the handle flying around like a windmill. Well, that's neither here nor there. I had in mind to roll this grindstone down past Mr. Guppy's front porch, and off into the front field, and then spend a good deal of time watching him go to all the work of getting it back into the shed again. As I say, I'm hazy on some of this now, but at the time it seemed like a good thing to do. So I got it rolling, like a hoop, and

I cuffed it along, and away we went right by Mr. Guppy's front porch.

"Now, how was I to know he'd be sitting out there in the dark, probably thinking up ways to be mean? But there he was; when I trotted by he sat up and took notice, and he also took after me. I had the thing going right along then, and the crank was flying around on the side away from me at a good clip. We hit one end of Mr. Guppy's hog fence, and wound up about thirty-five yards of it in the flying handle and you could hear staples pulling out if they pulled, and stakes coming out of the ground if they didn't. Mr. Guppy kept a steady flow of remarks which indicated disapproval, but I was too busy at the moment to reply.

"Then I hit the soft ground around his sink-spout drain and the grindstone sank in and there was a muddy conclusion to the pursuit. Mr. Guppy collared me, and he says, 'That looks like my grindstone!' I now realized deep inside that whatever had been in my mind in the beginning had not now panned out 100 per cent. Anyway, old man Guppy looked his grindstone over, and he said the edges had been chipped by this experience, and that if it was the last thing I ever did I was going to pay for it.

"I've never known, then or now, just what a grindstone is worth, new or secondhand. Money, then, was just something you touched briefly in the eighth grade under 'banking and currency' and proposing to a small boy that he ante up and pay money was wildest pretense. But Mr. Guppy and my father had a summit meeting, and then I agreed to hoe the corn for Mr. Guppy until the grindstone was paid for.

"It took two weeks. His corn patch ran from the main road back to Sandy Stream, and while I suppose it's half a mile it seemed to me then to be about the same distance as Utah. Every night he would tell me he was satisfied with my work, that I was doing well. And at the end of two very long weeks he said, 'There, now I figure the grindstone is paid for. Let that be a lesson to you, and you ought to be glad I was kind and lenient instead of making things hard on you!'

"So that night I hitched our old Meg into the wagon, and I drove over to Mr. Guppy's and began to load the grindstone into the wagon. I had a plank, and was rolling it up, and old man Guppy came out and took one look at me and he said, 'What do you think you're doing?' I said I was taking my grindstone home. He said I most certainly was not. I said I could if I wanted to, that it was mine and I'd paid for it, and I wanted it.

"Then old man Guppy went over to see my father, and I remember my father spoke very slowly, like a judge making a weighty decision, and he said, 'Now, Mr. Guppy, I don't want to appear to be defending the boy, but it seems to me you have been hoist on the price of your own grindstone. I'm inclined to think you were more concerned about getting your corn hoed than you were about reproving a wayward youngster. In the cross-wind of motives, you lost sight of the definitions. I suggest you take what it would cost to hire a man for two weeks, and go buy a new grindstone — and from here on I'll handle the boy.'

"And that's what happened. Old man Guppy had to go buy a new grindstone for haying season, and I still have the one I bought from him. It is chipped a little on the edges, but when I use it I make allowances, and I reflect on my misspent youth and the iniquities thereof."

THE TIMER LOOK

To us old-time tin-lizzie people, progress is often baffling. The way my garageman turns and looks at me, as if I had just arrived from Lapland and asked him to shoe a reindeer, is what I call the "timer look." I don't know just when the timer ceased to be part of the automobile, and I have no idea what takes its place, but I know my practiced old ear can listen to a motor and tell you when the timer needs tinkering — whether it has a timer or not. But when my automobile needs some timer attention, and I tell my garageman, he turns and looks at me.

I got the timer look again the other day when I drove in and told my garageman, "I'm shimmying!"

"You don't look it from this side," he said.

The old tin-lizzie used to shimmy, and progress has gone so far that today's garagemen never worked on a tin-lizzie, and never knew what shimmying was. Yet it was a recognized part of highway travel, caused by the informal nature of automotive construction, and anybody who drove or rode used the word without any reference to exotic dancing. There was a thing underneath called the wishbone, and it would aggravate a clavicle, or something, and the front wheels would wobble. On a dirt road this would set you sidewise, and while the rear-wheel brakes were taking you'd go off into somebody's oat field.

There was no particular shame in this. Today the Highway Safety Committee keeps everybody keyed up so you don't brag about going off the road. But a good shimmy was a recognized part of motoring, an adventure in itself. Some people told about going up the Mount Washington road, and some told about going over a stone wall in a shimmy. As a conversational item shimmying wasn't as good as a jackknife. Jackknifing was when the wheels, turned a-port, suddenly decided to go a-starboard. They would do this in the grand manner, digging in and throwing gravel skyward, and jerking the occupants out of their shirts. But both shimmying and jackknifing were caused by short takes and long stresses in the steering department, and they had the salutary effect of keeping the speed down. When you knew you might skitter out into an oat field at any unpredictable moment, you didn't open things up much.

Somebody amended the manufacturer's failures by offering a device that caught up the loose ends that caused shimmying. It didn't exactly stop shimmying; it merely made it more comfortable and less likely. The thing had long springs, and a prudent motorist who had invested in this precaution got a high-strung vibration that accompanied him down the road like a concert on a harp. And sometimes one of these springs would pull loose and with a *ta-wing-g-g* noise would shoot off into space, cutting down daisies as it went. But mostly, since in those times about everybody was his own mechanic, shimmying was controlled by tightening nuts now and then, keeping the speed around the high twenties, and remaining alert.

So here the other day when my new, modern

vehicle, out of a clear sky, shimmied and danced me into, hooray, an oat field, it was like meeting up with an old high-school classmate. Nothing like that had happened since 1923. I felt young again. With a fond, delighted expression I turned to my seatmate and said, "We shimmied!"

He said, "If you take a notion to rhumba, let me out."

But when I drove in and told my garageman I had shimmied, he gave me that old timer look and said, "Probably that new wheel needs balancing."

The timer on a tin-lizzie was, of course, the forerunner of what is now called the distributor. It was that part of the ignition system that kept the cylinders in sequence. It was situated forward on the engine, just abaft the fan, and the worst thing on the whole contrivance to get at. It was, moreover, the thing you had to get at most often. The timer was the most discussed topic of the motorist's day, and if anything went wrong the first thing you did was take off the timer and look at it. I have no doubt at one time or another the timer even caused shimmying.

The reason for this latter-day shimmying, on a modern, new model, turned out to be a little silly. I'd been having a soft tire every second or third morning, and the garageman would look at it and put it back on, and he said there was no leak in it. So one morning

I was looking over his shoulder while he tried to solve this mystery, and I said, "Well, no wonder it goes soft — you haven't put any tube in it!"

He gave me the old timer look and explained that this was a tubeless tire. And I wasn't really ready for this, because I can remember how we'd put a tube over a mudguard and patch it out along the highway, and after we got patches on all the patches we'd still get a hundred thousand miles from a tube. When they began making automobiles without mudguards and running boards a fellow had no place to patch a tube any more, and they had to invent the tubeless tire. Timers and mudguards left us about the same time. So I said, "Well, if the rubber isn't leaking, maybe the steel rim is." He gave me the timer look again, but he went and got a pail of water and splashed it over the wheel — and sure enough, the steel wheel was porous.

"Never heard of such a thing!" he said.

"You never heard of a timer, either," I contributed. Then I said, making the most of things, "Maybe we could squeeze in some Never-Leak!"

I had to buy a new wheel, of course. There are a great many things on modern automobiles you can't take off and fix over a mudguard. And then I got the shimmy, and the whole thing bothers me. Well, the rubber people work their heads to the bone to develop a tubeless tire, and when it is perfected the automobile people put it on a porous wheel, and the result is a shimmy just like 1923 — when tires had tubes in them. Progress can be baffling.

The modern solution was the balancing of the wheel. The man told me he had a new machine that cost him three hundred and seventy-five dollars, and it would balance the new wheel right up nice. "That means," I said, "that you sold me a crooked wheel!" He gave me that timer look. "Why didn't you balance it before you sold it to me?"

"You do it after," he said.

My garageman, of course, thinks I know nothing at all about motor vehicles. In his smug possession of the lingo and jargon and sales talk he is superior. He can give me that timer look when I come in and say, "She's humping on the hills, better titivate the timer." That withering, pitying, disgusted look. Anyway, I told him to go fly a kite, that I wasn't going to pay him for balancing a new wheel that replaced a porous one, tube or no tube. "Don't you dare put 'wheel balancing' on my bill," I said.

And he didn't, either. My whole foray against the tire, rim and balance program came precisely to naught. There was no wheel balancing on my bill.

[93]

Instead, about halfway down, it said, most delightfully, "To adjust timer, $84.27."

I'm going to go in and give him an old timer look.

LONG PANTS AND LONGER MEMORIES

A fashion decree from Moscow says men's trousers will be shorter and tighter, although it doesn't say on which end. Whether or not the world is yet ready to take its styles from the Soviet remains to be seen, but if so, then I'm ready. I have a suit which is as short and as tight as any law will allow, and it's in fairly good condition. It hangs on a nail upstairs in the barn and is covered with a cotton feed bag. The feed bag isn't in bad condition either.

This suit happens to be the first suit I ever owned; the raiment that changed me from a boy to a man. I was about fifteen then; boys didn't get clapped into long-legged suits the minute they could climb from the playpen. Boys used to wear boys' clothes until they showed some disposition to mature. You didn't get a sport jacket and slacks on your second birthday. You acted like a man when you began to be one.

Does anybody remember how they used to pay men's wages and boys' wages? One day the foreman would call you aside and tell you he was now putting you on men's wages, and it meant you had accomplished something the likes of which no modern boy can understand. It would be all right now if you put on long pants. Symbolically, you could stand in a potato basket and hold up two sacks of potatoes. A big moment.

So, by some standard I had reached that moment, and we sent word to Mr. Osgood, who came over to the house one evening. Mr. Osgood had the agency in our town. He brought a book of swatches and a tape measure, and while engaging in pleasant conversation with the family about all manner of things he went around me like a cooper around a barrel, and he put all my sizes down on an order form. Afterwards, all the family turned to and helped select the cloth. In those days a new suit cost fourteen dollars, and it was no light and transient matter to choose the fabric. Suits didn't grow on trees, and it would be a long time before I got another. We wanted something that would wear.

The color ought to be about right, too, because a young man cutting his first figure at a sociable should avoid the frivolous. We chose a decent brown, with a kind of sandy or cornmeal grain to it that highlighted the restraint. It had a faint pencil stripe as well, which accented the vertical.

As the ultimate consumer in this deal, I was supposed to have my choice of suspenders or belt, gratis. But Mother decided suspenders would be more graceful. She called them galluses, and was against belts because they might shut off your wind. Mother never liked belts and was able always to think up some good reason. Mr. Osgood diplomatically offered that galluses were generally more popular at that time, so with this assurance I felt all right about choosing suspenders, although I really wanted a belt.

I was astonished when the suit came by parcel post from Chicago. We had studied about Chicago in geography, but I didn't suppose Mr. Osgood would have any connection with a place so far away. A little note in the box thanked us for our custom and said if the fitting wasn't satisfactory to get in touch with "our representative." That was Mr. Osgood. The fit, however, was a dandy. It was a dream. I wore it first to a strawberry time and was the belle of the ball. Everybody spoke of the nice fit and the attractive weave, and several said, unbelieving, "You didn't get *that* from Mr. Osgood, did you!" At closing exercises in school that June I was a beautiful thing in my new suit, and then I put it on a hanger in my closet and spent the summer making hay. By fall I was several hands higher, and no longer the proportioned vision Mr. Osgood had so carefully fitted. I took down the suit for the first social event of the fall season, and my feet stuck out of the pants as if I were on stilts. My hands dangled from the sleeves like paddles on a string. The vest was so tight my eyes bulged.

But that suit had cost fourteen whole dollars and I was stuck with it. I had to alternate the two pairs of pants faithfully so I might get the longest possible good from the investment, and when I elected to repeat the sad story of Philip Nolan in the prize speaking contest the next spring I hit the high spot of my considerable career. The hilarity I engendered was not in keeping with the high drama of the story.

Instead of weeping for poor Nolan, my audience whooped and cheered, and all I needed to go on the Orpheum circuit was a black paper patch over my front teeth. When I gestured culturally to indicate the deep remorse that flooded the unfortunate hero's saddened soul, my hand swept the sky like a comet and this took up my other armpit so I jerked myself into a spasm. I had rehearsed all this in a sweater.

So, I was stuck with it. The pants got let down to the last thread. The waistband had a gusset, and the gusset had a gore. The vest was ripped up the back so I could button the front, and the coat was now so tight through the back that the side pockets were up under my ears. I wore that suit until both pairs of pants became unstable, and after they were discreetly patched I wore them some more.

But at last it was time for my second suit. My first one was more than too small now, and I was staying home rather than wear it. I hung it in the closet for good, and found the price of suits had gone up to sixteen dollars and a half. And that was with just one pair of pants. I understand they are even higher now. And one day after I had retired my first long-legged suit I found it over a chair downstairs, and Mother said she was going to hook it into a rug. I put my foot down and said I guessed I'd keep my first suit because of fond memories. I took it up in the barn, where I keep my treasures safe.

But if Moscow decrees tight pants, I've got just the thing. Those pants, last time I had them on, were so tight I couldn't wink to play Winkum, and when you are sixteen or seventeen this is not good. Shall we await further word from abroad?

DOGGEREL BY THE QUART

Occasionally things of an abstruse and intellectual nature thrust themselves upon me, and when they touch on rural matters I give them my attention. I have here "some literature" (namely, a catalog) pricing new milk bottles, and I'm wondering who writes the poetry on them. I suppose we could even drop back a notch behind that and wonder why poetry appears on milk bottles at all, but probably the surging tide of American culture has rolled so far that we'll gain nothing by considering that. The Greeting Card, alone, is too big an industry for the likes of us to ponder, now, the subtler aspects of the functional rhyme.

The truth is, that when I pick up a volume of loved and lasting poetry and settle back with contemplative and relaxed attention, I know full well I am doing something that has gone out of style in our day and age, but if I chance upon some jewel of thought, something woven of moonbeams and gardenias, I always feel repaid. But no such sentient awareness envelopes me when I pick up the quart milk bottle and read:

> *Here are two kids*
> *Chuck full of glee,*
> *They like our milk*
> *It's plain to see.*

Great and good poetry doth stimulate the mind, but even the ponderous latinity of John Milton doesn't tease me as I am teased now — whatever possessed somebody to work up this jingle and imprint it on glass? In the field of written communication the jingle is certainly a smallish matter when compared to the line next below: *Please wash and return bottles daily.* Why does a milkman feel that the healthy nourishment of cow's milk requires a jingle? And, of course, this is a minor sample of the flux of similar doggerel that besets the jinglingest, and least poetic, era in history.

I find the poet is not particularly esteemed, really. You introduce a poet to somebody, and say, "He's a poet," and people look at him as if he were odd and suspect. Publishers shy from manuscripts of poetry. "It doesn't sell," say the bookstores. Yet anybody who has ever edited anything, from significant chapbooks down to Professor La Figue's Almanac, knows that every mail brings verses from people who fancy they are poets and who spend time whipping odd and random thoughts into rhythmic expression. One editor, not long ago, thrust his tongue into his cheek and paid for and printed an apostrophe to the lily, and readers were rewarded as follows:

> *The soil for onions rank,*
> *Is fine for lilies, too —*
> *Some don't like onions much,*
> *Others do.*

Saunders

The explanation of this is easy. Somebody, immersed in the humdrum of everyday cares, sought solace in poetic creation, and without knowing the fundamentals of a difficult art came up with sawn and split rhyme which couched an absurdity in the validity of what appeared to be form. And these people, being able to turn out go-star-dough-far and kids-glee-milk-see by the quart and gallon are the ones who ignore and tread down the careful scanner who labors six months on a single word and still feels he hasn't got it right.

You find, if you look closely enough, that some of the thoughts attempted by these milk-bottle songsters are really good thoughts, and if expressed in rudimentary prose they might attract the attention of the philosophers. But thinking they must jingle to make it good, they try the twinkle-twinkle-little-star routine and peter out trying to find a rhyme for some word like surcingle, or raspberry.

Then there are the people who write sonnets to accompany a frying pan that is a gift at a kitchen shower, permitting a real poet to run a gasoline station down on the corner because he has no patronage for his pinioned flecks of beauty against the azure sky. While poets pump gasoline, somebody turns out a jingle for a milk bottle and has to make two trips a day to the bank, Monday through Friday.

Evidently the public sees a big difference between "They like our milk, it's plain to see," and, "It's plain to see they like our milk." The simple, direct, straightforward expression of a basic thought is twisted to accommodate the verse, coming out backwards in the necessity of rhyme. This conveys an illusion of labor, I suppose, and in a poet it would be called bathos, but on a milk bottle it's good. Only with tongue in cheek would an editor accept such, and then he would feel a little guilty about perpetrating a hoax — but the milkman cometh and payeth good money and is glad.

It's not just the milkman, of course. We're all parties to it. So long as the public has so little discernment, the jingles will run on. A rebirth of learning, perhaps... Possibly the real poets of the future, the Brownings and Swinburnes and Keatses, will work this market and we will find things like the Grecian Urn on a vinegar jug. Somehow I don't like this prospect.

Maybe the literary critique, as a guide to the tastes of the public, needs to broaden its base. Magazines and newspapers that assay the output of real poets need to begin evaluating the milk-bottle jingles and other jaunts to Parnassus such as greeting cards, hash recipes and the labels on snow shovels. In time, with care, a few people might come to know that Paradise Lost is one thing and a quart of Grade A Homogenized is another.

IMPROVING THE SILENCE

Every once in a while somebody will put a harness vise on a piano, and explain that it is a conversational piece. In my opinion, conversation that has to be prompted and prodded by such props isn't usually worth the candle, and I was glad to have this opinion confirmed when Dr. Plummer dropped in not long ago and took supper. The Doc was then in his eighties, mostly retired from a lifetime of country practice. An institution in our town, he had been around longer than anybody, and as a conversationalist he had no peer.

Equipped with broad reading that was by no means limited to professional topics, he was ready to take any side in a discussion, and he never joined any company without enhancing its intellectual batting average. The most unnecessary thing in the world, with Doc, was a knickknack intended to stir up talk.

Doc told about a stranger who came into town and tried to make conversation with a number of people, but couldn't seem to get anything much going. Finally he asked, "What is there, a law around here against talk?"

"No," said one of the natives. "But we do have a

kind of mutual agreement amongst us that nobody says anything unless he can improve on the silence."

One time long years ago, now, the Doc was pushing his horse on a call up at Peppermint Corner, and he went past a house where a chimney fire had just set some shingles ablaze. The old lady who lived in the house was a dedicated recluse, and not much was known about her. She didn't come to the door when the Doc thumped with the butt of his buggy whip, but he could see her peeping from behind the shutters. He pounded some more, and she opened the portal just a crack.

"Your house is on fire!" the Doc shouted.

And the old lady said, "Is that all?"

"Well," said the Doc, "that's all I think of right now."

That evening at supper Doctor Plummer covered numerous topics. He told how he went to Augusta one time to speak in favor of a bill at a legislative hearing, and he found the place was full of people who were all on his side. But he was the only one who said anything. Afterwards everybody came up and congratulated him on his remarks, and said they were with him 100 per cent and he had done a fine job. Doc said the committee voted unanimously against the bill, and it made him feel like Winkelried, who bunched the spears of the opposition and heroically absorbed the entire defense.

Then the Doc told about a radio program he had listened to, where Groucho Marx was giving away all kinds of money to people who answered his questions, and a considerable fortune was riding on the name of Adam's third son. Doc said the chance to get rich quick was muffed completely, and that he considered this a great reprimand to the culture of our nation, which spends all outdoors on education to turn out people who can't answer questions any educated person should be able to.

Doc said the literary heritage that comes down to us, quite apart from the sacred aspects, ought to give us a planned culture in which any mature person should be able to answer certain elementary questions such as Adam's third son, who built the Ark, who pulled down the temple, and things like that. Doc thought Groucho Marx should have seized the opportunity to stimulate inquiry and interest, not only to promulgate knowledge but to rebuke people for not knowing something they ought to know. The quiz program, Doc said, rewards those who know, but it doesn't send the masses hurrying out to inform themselves.

Doc thought Groucho might have expounded briefly on Seth, and opened vistas for the ignorant.

Doc said, "You know, the story of a man like Seth is an interesting thing. He was in a tough spot. He came along after the main event, an afterthought, and as soon as he arrived his paw took a look at him and remarks that here is somebody who can take Abel's place. Bang, like that, his whole life was dedicated to filling a blank. Not the best kind of billing. Poor Seth. I think it makes Adam look a little unkind, and certainly not altogether smart. I sat there listening to the radio, and I got kind of angry at Groucho Marx — he missed a good chance."

Then somehow Doc got off on another tack and told how the town, years ago, had hired an old seafaring man to erect a flagpole in the square. He came with his crew and a yoke of oxen and got everything in readiness. The long spruce staff, with a topmast, stretched up the street, with the big hole in the ground at its foot, and in our highlander town this nautical job attracted a big crowd to see. Just as the old sea captain was about to give orders to hoist away, somebody from the non-tidal community called out, "Y'ain't got your rope in!"

He referred to the rope that would raise and lower the flag through a pulley at the masthead, which hadn't been attached yet, and would be much harder to attach after the pole was up. The old mariner tossed an indignant look at this interruption, raised his hand and called, "Hoist away!"

"But your rope ain't in!"

"Hoist away!"

Then somebody else, perceiving that the semantic block was at loggerheads — and I suppose it was Doc who did this — was able to bring two points of view into focus by crying out, "Hey, Skipper, ain't you goin' to reeve your single halyard?"

That did it. The boss man lowered his hand, looked at the pole, threaded his rope through the pulley, and the job went ahead.

As Doc said, it isn't quite enough to have something to say, you've got to know how to say it so it will get across. Doc went home in the shank of the evening, and as he went out the door I told him he had greatly improved the silence. I could see this pleased him.

SHAKESPOKES AND THE MONSTER

Out here in the country some of us are pleased that our literary pursuits run apace. Our Shakespeare Club, for instance, is well over fifty years old and those who belong to it dedicate one evening a week to culture of the highest kind. They even have a charter member. The husbands of members refer to them flippantly as Shakespokes, and as husbands they take part in some of the activities, as well as glean considerable top-notch polish just by being exposed.

Well, one of the club's customs, by no means limited to this club, is to answer roll call by contributing a pithy saying, memory gem, and quite often a quotation from Shakespeare — and a husband benefits from this greatly. Just as his wife is putting on her hat to rush off to meeting, she will say, "Oh, I forgot — roll call! Tell me something Shakespeare said about fortitude!"

It has been my custom for some years now, on Shakespeare evenings, to go up to Mel Smith's house, and we belabor the cribbage board together until the Bard has adjourned. Usually, at noon, Mel will call on the telephone to see if the plans are steadfast, and I got up from my chicken soup expecting him to be there when I answered the ring. The night before I had been reading a magazine piece that dealt with telephone manners, and it said altogether too few people spoke into the instrument the proper way. We should be more melodic in our articulations, it said, and develop geniality and warmth. So I said hello in a manner that suggested honey dripping from the comb, salubrious summer zephyrs wafting from bowers of roses, and the essence of genteel bonhomie.

It was Mel's wife, Ernestine. "What in the world is the matter with you?" she said.

"I was reading a magazine," I said. "It says that a pleasant voice over the telephone will make even a bill collector's day happy and joyful. I was practicing."

"Oh," she said. "I thought I had the wrong number. Who slew the monster?"

"Not I," I said. "I didn't even vote for him."

"Vote for who . . . whom?" said Ernestine.

So I said, "Now, wait a minute. You started this. I was sitting here minding my own business, and the telephone rang. Remember? What are you talking about?"

"I'm talking about the monster in the maze. Who slew him?"

"I haven't seen the paper today," I said. "Did it happen here in town?"

"Oh, cut it out!" said Ernestine. "Isn't your cook going to Shakespeare?"

"Of course she is. She always does."

"Well, this is for roll call. Who slew the monster in the maze at Crete?"

"Fine," I said. "Now we have established rapport, and I am conversant with the details. I find that the subject for tonight is Grecian mythology, and at this

[109]

late hour my best neighbor's favorite wife hasn't done her homework. Shame on you."

"Look," said Ernestine, "I don't have much time, and I need to know who slew the Minotaur!"

"Good evening," I said, imitating the magazine about telephonic amenities. "This is your Answer-Man, drop a coin in the slot and state your query. There will be a brief pause whilst the oracle is consulted and the entrails have been inspected. Go ahead, please!"

Ernestine said, "Look, you nut, do you or don't you?"

"Yes," I said, "I do. I do, indeed. But I am not a member of the Shakespokes . . ."

"Shakespeares," she said.

". . . Shakespokes, and there is no reason for me to show concern. I have some books down here, and if you care to avail yourself . . ."

Ernestine then devoted a few moments to the kind of telephone conversation the magazine distinctly rejected.

"Was it Hercules?" I said.

"No," she said. "It wasn't Hercules."

"Was it Heriklitekon?"

"Who's he?"

"He runs a banana store in Providence, Rhode Island," I said.

Well, to make a short story long, we ran down the boatloads of maidens going out from Athens, old King Minos, Ariadne and the ball of twine, Daedalus and Icarus, and I got a little mileage out of the House of Atreus. Day to day, you don't get much call around here for Greek mythology, and I made the most out of all this.

I said, "This is wonderful, I haven't thought about all those old yarns in a long time. I'm grateful."

Ernestine said, "But who slew the monster?"

"Theseus," I said.

"Well, why didn't you say so!"

Later that evening Ernestine's husband and I were still pegging away at cribbage when the two Shake-spokes came in, reporting that all had gone well and the roll call had been a huge success. Tantalus was still in trouble, the springs of Ida still gush, and the lotus eaters are getting plenty of lotuses. "Sounds as if things are in good shape," I said. "Tell me, how is Prince Hal these days?"

"Prince who?" they both said, and the only reason I dwell on all this is to show you that all is not haying and milking on a farm, but now and then the deep running stream of culture laves our bucolic lives.

THE BROODY BIRD

        Of all the phenomena available to the observant agronomist, the mantle of motherhood as it descends upon the feathered kind is the most fun. All of us do foolish things, from time to time, and as imagination is vouchsafed us we explain them as best we can. But the broody bird explains nothing, and with inborn genius does things inherently which are far better than even the most ingenious of us could invent. It is a great wonder to me, the way birds act, that their species is advanced at all. This year's crop of bird-on-the-nest stories is as good as ever.

We had a Granite State Rock (advt.) who decided to set. Grammarians must concede that with hens sitting is setting. Calvin Coolidge said that whether or not a hen is lying or laying is discovered by picking her up to find out, and when a hen sits she sets. Biologically hens can't sit, and grammatically they can't set, so you have to give a little, take a little. Anyway, this hen spent the usual time getting ready, during which everybody knew what she was about but she thought they didn't, and she made a mighty leap of about fourteen feet into the haymow. Then she sought out a special place along the edge of the mow and she scootched down and ruffled her feathers and wiggled around until she had made a dandy nest in the hay. Having thus created a receptacle, she laid an egg in it.

What she had done in the magnificent stupidity that comes to birds touched with the maternal urge was to wiggle so much that she had gone right down through the hay until she had come to the two spruce poles most nearly under her, the supports for the mow, and she had centered her effort upon the gap between them. If you had gone aloft and gazed at her, you would have seen a hen on a very fine nest, but if you had gone in below and looked up you would have seen part of a hen through a little space between two logs. This was the situation that prevailed when she thought all was in readiness and she laid her first egg.

I wasn't there, and I don't know everything, but I presume the egg hit the tie-up floor beneath with unerring accuracy, and lay there (observe the pun!) in an inert fashion. I further presume that Stubbie, our cat, found this egg during the regular night patrol, and because Stubbie likes hen's eggs Stubbie ate it. Stubbie thrust the shell aside as unsalable. By the time I found out what was going on Stubbie had a big pile of shells and had worn the plank down by lapping eggs. As I wondered what had caused this erosion and debris I looked up, and I observed my hen partially between the poles, and realized that impending motherhood was thwarted. I put the hen in a broody coop, and she is fine, now.

At the same time one of our lady ducks decided to brood, and with the wisdom of the feathered kind she selected a bare spot on the ground right where our dooryard slopes off into the orchard. I found her there one morning, and she had eight eggs. That was three weeks ago, and since it takes four weeks to hatch duck eggs she has been sliding down the hill at the rate of about eight feet a night and has twenty-eight more feet to go.

A duck builds her nest after she has one. That is, she picks a spot and lays an egg, and then she begins building. She pulls down from her body, picks up twigs and straw, and weaves an intricate nest as she goes — and in this instance she is going right along. Every night she lays another egg, and tears the nest apart and remakes it in a new place. She could have selected a level spot, but she didn't. This is about par for the feathered course. She is hatching her young on the run.

Close study shows this sort of absurdity is not for the barnyard kind, alone. I've been watching a mother robin, and she is unhappy and bewildered, and I don't know if she'll make it or not. She has nested on the handle of a shovel. I had an old barn shovel, for cleaning out hog pens, and I put it up under the beam of the barn, blade first, so the handle sticks out into the atmosphere. No reason to do this that way, nor any reason to do it another. I didn't have robins in mind. So the hand-grip part of the handle must have looked like a fork in an apple tree, and this old biddy robin came along and built a nest there.

I didn't know anything about it, but one morning this hen robin came barreling out from under the barn with a rude squawk, and she perched in a tree and combed me out in a most unfriendly manner. I would not care to repeat the things she said. I blushed for several minutes. In the next few days she did this now and then, and I investigated to see what was causing such unrest among the tenants.

It was simple enough. The shovel blade was up under a floorboard, and the board was loose. Whenever anybody stepped into the grainroom up on the main floor of the barn they walked on this board, and this made the shovel handle vibrate. The old lady would be tossed out of her nest, but it wasn't quite enough action to throw the eggs out, too. In the depths of preoccupation that absorbs the feathered female during the gestation period, she would be hunched there in repose, one eye staring into a knot-hole, and all at once she would be ejected. After a few moments of vituperation and calumny she would return, and as long as there was nobody going or coming in the grainroom incubation went ahead nicely. You can't reason with birds.

But I often think I could hatch eggs after a better plan.

SWALLOWS IN THE SUNSET

Whenever the sun sets as it did tonight, in a welter of high color, somebody always says, "Yes, and if an artist painted it, you'd say it wasn't real." I wouldn't, myself, really, because I like to be kind to artists. I've even praised some things now and then when I haven't been sure, and I think a painter should be praised for even contemplating a sunset. But I will go along with the general idea, that sunsets are beyond the possibilities.

You can't paint a sunset for the very good reason that there's more to it than paint and proportion. The splash of a sunset's color beguiles us, and we come home thinking there was nothing there except the color. Hearing and feeling are overwhelmed. I've long felt most people miss most of a sunset, because all they remember are the reds and golds and purples.

I had a row of beets one year that ran off into new ground, and the weeds got ahead of me. It was a matter of doing something or goodbye beets, so after supper I went down in the cool of the day and picked away at them. It had been a hot day, and just the kind for a ripping good sunset, and I knew one was making up when the little weeds at the end of my fingers began looking the same color as the beets. A few mosquitoes came around, which goes with that time of day, but my blood is thin and about all they do is look in my ears and go tch, tch. It was time to quit.

I tossed the hoe over my shoulder and turned toward the house — facing into the sunset and seeing it all at once in its magnificence. It really was a good one. I thought the color was judiciously disposed, running heavily to about everything, and it embraced a panoply or two which stacked up among the best. A thin haze was hugging the horizon to make the sun a great globe of pure red, even better than the beets in the catalog. Long mares' tails were fetching this up into the banks of mackerel sky so everybody would get a chance to see it. And I think that's about where an artist would have to stop.

You couldn't exactly paint in the age-old meaning of mares' tails and mackerel sky, which are sure-fire harbingers of wet weather. You couldn't paint in the tree frogs that I could hear trilling from the orchard — little suction cups on their feet had taken them up into the limbs, and now they were corroborating the cloud formation. Tree frogs trilling in the dusk mean rain. You couldn't paint in the robins, either, who were calling for rain. A pleasant summer shower brings the earthworms up onto the lawn, and a robin begs for moisture when the sun is going down. Anybody might think it would storm.

But a fine sunset like this one, according to the old observations, is itself a promise of fair weather. Fair and hot. Tomorrow would be a beautiful day, excellent for haying. A positive promise. So what do you do with the conflicting auguries, and do you go by the ball of red fire in the haze, or heed the mackerel sky? "In dry times, all signs fail," comes to mind. My guess was for good weather.

That was because the swallows were flying high. They were dipping, wheeling, arching, plunging — and chattering — through the fire of the sky, at times splashing off great rubies as they flew. Swallows flying high are a sign of good weather. But it's not really on their own account — a lot of things in this world are like that. You see a lot of people who appear to be doing well, and then you find they inherited a fortune and a house on the lake front. The swallows don't fly high because it is going to be good weather. You look up, and they seem to be opinionating, and you quote, "Swallows high, hot and dry!" That might

[118]

be a good title, come to think of it, for a sunset painting.

But the truth is that the swallows are just the victims of a common worldly urge, and they fly high because they are hungry. They are up there because the bugs are up there. How they can wheel and dart in the fading light and catch bugs at top speed is something to marvel at, but they do it, and they will be at it long after your own eyesight loses them. The bugs are up there for reasons of their own, and we are on an ad infinitum excursion.

Barometric pressure, of course — conditions that bring on good weather are conditions that make bugs fly high. It's as simple as that, but nobody could paint it into a sunset. It's like apple blossoms and trout. Trout begin to take when the orchards are in bloom, but it isn't simple cause and effect. Trout don't know when the blossoms open. But the weather conditions that open the buds are the same conditions that hatch flies along the brook, and the trout respond just as the swallows do — to old-fashioned appetite. It's most unpoetic, and not paintable. The apple bloom has nothing to do with it, except that you notice it and are reminded. So with the swallows flying high — it would be a good day tomorrow.

But now the sun was gone. The last touch of red had gone below the treetops on the Ridge, and the air cooled. You could feel the difference at once. And a light dusk breeze stirred the meadow grasses, already wet with the new dew. Why does the air always stir when the sun goes down, and with the changing of the tide? Has some physicist formulated a theory we could put into a painting? Curtains shift at the windows, smoke swirls at the chimney, and then everything is still again. An exact point.

So, it was a sunset all right, and when I got to the house they said, "Did you see the sunset?" And that's it. From house windows you can only *see* a sunset, and what he can see is what an artist can paint. That's a small part of it, thinks I.

ANYONE FOR HINKY-PINKY?

A "left-handed diplomat" is, quite naturally, a "sinister minister," and if it's never happened before you have now been introduced to the game of hinky-pinky, which is a wonderful sport to entertain the young ones while riding in an automobile. It came as a surprise to me, too, and I've found it can do for you what "Punch, Brothers, Punch" did for Mark Twain.

I don't always keep up with affairs, just as affairs

don't sometimes keep up with me, so I was unready. We had taken Sunday afternoon off and had driven into Kennebago to call on our friends the Russells, and after watching the sun set in splendor behind the West Kennebago Range, the lake incarnadined, we started home again.

The first nine miles, which lie over a dirt road through the wilderness, were spent watching for animals, and after that I supposed Kathie had curled up on the back seat to snooze. But as we coasted down the seven miles off the height of land into Madrid (Maine, that is), she suddenly said out of the rear-end darkness, "This is a hinky-pinky — high water!"

"We'll be home in an hour," I said soothingly. "You can get a drink then."

"No," she said. "This is a hinky-pinky — high water!"

"It's a game," my wife said.

"High water," said Kathie.

"A big swig?" asked my wife.

"No," said Kathie. "Hinky-pinky, not hink-pink."

"Oh," said my wife.

We were now coming into Madrid.

As we went out of Madrid, somewhat simultaneously for Madrid is not large, my wife said, "Is it an upper cup o'?"

"No," said Kathie. "That's silly."

"Look," I said. "Is there some law against telling me what's going on?"

They filled me in as we wound down along Sandy River. This pastime consists of thinking up two rhymed words, such as "frail snail," and then you give a synonym definition such as "tender univalve." If your rhyming words have one syllable apiece, it's a hink-pink. For two apiece, it's hinky-pinky, and if you can muster three apiece, it's hinkety-pinkety. So everybody exhausts all the possibilities until somebody says frail-snail, and then everybody says, "Oh, that was a good one!"

So we were hinky-pinkying with high water.

About the time we hit the cut-off at Phillips I said, "Great spate!"

"No," said Kathie. "I keep telling you it's a hinky-pinky."

So we gave up.

"Mountain fountain," she said.

We said, "Oh, that's a good one!"

Next came wiggley tree, which was a loose spruce.

Then we did cowardly gentleman, which was a yellow fellow.

Then extra bunny, which was a spare hare.

By this time we were going through Farmington and I decided to try my hand at this intellectual exercise. "Prevaricating king," I said, and silence settled over our journey until we were down to North Livermore. They not only didn't guess it; they didn't even venture a trial. It was peaceful riding along in the dark in silence.

I got to thinking about the fine summer people we had met at Kennebago Lake, and how nice it is to live in a state that appeals so much to folks wishing to escape briefly from the rigors of city life, and how pretty the sunset had been, and I reflected along by myself until somebody said, "I give up!"

"What's the matter?" I asked.

"We give up."

"Give up what?"

"The hinky-pinky."

I had to confess my thoughts had wandered until I couldn't recall what it was. "What was it?" I asked.

"The prevaricating king."

"Oh, yes," I said. "That was an easy one. Prevaricating king. Lyin' lion!"

"Oh, that's not fair! We were thinking about Henry the Eighth and Charlemagne, and MacKenzie King, and checkers, and things like that there!"

"The lion is the king of beasts," I said. "And for our present purposes we assume that he has fibbed to the queen, who is a lioness. It is all legal and proper. Now I will give you another one."

We were just coming into Turner, and I said, "Artificial whale!"

Silence ensued, and we came to our own driveway in a consummate hush. "You can get out," I said. "We're home."

"What is an artificial whale?" they said.

"Rubber blubber," I said, and they allowed that they wouldn't play that game again with me. Which is all right with me, but the next morning as I started for the garden I turned back into the kitchen and said, "A larger ceiling!" I can see, as the days unfold, that they are reluctant to raise the subject again. They would like to know, but they don't say anything. If they ever ask me, and I haven't forgotten, the answer is "Vaster plaster."

That's a good one, and in the meantime I am making them up and storing them away. I've got three or four that should be good for forty miles apiece on the highway, and I shall spring them as occasion requires. One of my best is a hinketyhink-pinketypink. I'm just waiting. It is "military band."

That should hold them a long time. It's a regimental instrumental. Oh, that's a good one!

GRRR ON GOURMETS

By the rarest good chance I learned recently that dog biscuits now come in six delicious flavors — milk, meat, chicken, cheese, vegetable and liver. Our dog hasn't found out about this yet, and this reminds me of the ancient vaudeville routine:

"My dog doesn't eat beefsteak!"
"Your dog doesn't eat beefsteak?"
"No, my dog doesn't eat beefsteak."
"Why doesn't your dog eat beefsteak?"
"We don't give him any."

I have been a student of dogs ever since I can remember, and I would say I was all of four when I first discovered that their gastronomic versatility and catholicity of taste render it relatively unimportant what you give them to eat, just so long as it is food. At that time I had a dog named Louie, who was to achieve the distinction of being stolen from me by the chief of police. This can be substantiated, although it isn't always credited.

Anyway, I had a seersucker suit, white elk sandals and a flat straw hat — a rig that my mother thought was the height of style. She had some relatives at a distance and she wanted to show them how well she was doing, so she garbed me in these monstrosities and pushed my go-cart across town to a kitchen-photographer who made up some postcards. At the time I was most sensitive about wearing those things, and none of this feeling has diminished since. Somebody now and then brings out one of those postcards and I get the feeling all over again. But at the time I somehow communicated this feeling to Louie.

Louie was named for the Louis Frothingham who then was Lieutenant Governor of Massachusetts, and he had done some political maneuver that my father either approved or disapproved. The Frothingham pedigree ran high, but our Louie was one of the most complete and thorough mongrels ever concocted. He ate my straw hat. Just what flavor it was is lost to us now, but Louie ate it and I quietly sat by and observed the ingestion and thought it was a splendid idea. Mother arrived when Louie was about half done, and she let him eat the rest of it, possibly hoping there might be some adverse effect. Mother wasn't as keen on Louie as I was.

Since then I have seen dogs eat a great many things, and not one of the procession we've had here on the farm has ever had any special dietary concessions that might teach him expensive habits. None of them has ever wasted away, either. Some of them have even got fat without our really contributing that well.

We had one that wouldn't touch a thing we put in his pan, but he got so fat he couldn't go under the table to sleep. One time he showed up with a slab of smoked pork loin about three feet long, indicating he had access to a market somewhere, and we always told people he was the dog that brought home the bacon. Somebody told us once that a really good dog would eat only at his own dish, but this dog never went to his own dish and he was a good dog and discharged his domestic obligations faithfully and in top-notch fashion.

So I would say that in the broad vista there is a lot of notionality about what and how dogs eat. Evidently people like to impute human sensitivities and perceptions to the pooch, and because a man likes cheese he thinks his dog shares this enthusiasm. He may or may not, and he will probably eat it without really knowing, but we do seem to arrive at our conclusion through the master, not through the dog. True, we don't have any easy way to ask the dog and get a considered answer, but to imply that the hound is unhappy unless he has a crack at six delicious flavors is going too far, because we do know that doggie responses depend, sometimes, on other than appetite and taste.

Well, we had two pups once, Mephistopheles and Mrs. Topheles, and they hated bannock. We used to bake off great sheets of bannock for them because it is supposed to be good for hounds, and they hated it. They would turn up their noses and sneer at it and back away — so long as only one of them was there at a time. But you let both of them arrive at their respective dishes of bannock at the same time, and each would be afraid that the other was going to get it all, and they'd clean up any amount of bannock. The bannock would disappear so fast there was no possible chance to tell if it was meat, milk, chicken, cheese, vegetable or liver. That shows how it is with dogs.

If a dog doesn't have all the creature comforts designed for human beings, it doesn't necessarily follow that he is being cruelly used. They deserve a kind home that keeps decent hours and sets a good table, in return for which they contribute generously in their own way, but they don't need baskets to sleep in and ribbons in their hair, or even regular baths. They don't *need* them, and now and then a dog will say so. I doubt if six delicious dog flavors would be hailed as a triumphal idea if there weren't any humans to hail it.

Nobody has ever had more fun with dogs than I, or ever had any nicer dogs, but I've never tried to im-

pose on them over and beyond their natural disposi-
tions, and it isn't really hard to figure out what dogs
are like. You're only a dog once, and you ought to
have your head.

I don't say there's anything wrong with six delicious flavors. I think we might ponder, however, on
what they are, and why a dog biscuit company
selects these six to the exclusion of six others. If the
family is eating beef stew, that's the flavor a dog seems
to prefer at that moment, but if it comes to his plate
compounded with a little peanut butter, sour milk
biscuits, a laving of milk, some Indian meal pudding
and a dab of boiled cabbage he'll eat it. On most
farms, being fed as well as that, he'll eat it or go
hungry until he does. And although a farm dog probably has milk, meat, chicken, cheese, vegetable and
liver from time to time, he probably also has them
once in a while all at once, with ice cream and pic-
calilli, and goes out afterwards and hunts for a wood-
chuck without really knowing what it was.

Knowing dogs as I do, I'd suggest in humility that
somebody bring out six delicious dog flavors based
on dogs – not on humans. I would suggest Old Rubber Boot, Hog Trough Patina, Meat Market Back
Door, Lace Curtain, Anything in the Cat's Dish, and
Conglomerate Goodies. A dog, I think would like
that. A dog, that is, not a patsy.

TAKING COWS TO PASTURE

The big news in dairy circles, at one point, was that the Allessio Brothers of Pittsfield, Massachusetts, had stopped taking their cows to pasture and were now bringing the pasture to the cows. When I heard that I said, "There, now!" Shortly, "zero pasturage" was a common term and cows were left in the barn, or stood on bare barnyard dirt, while a mechanized management toted them their provender. Farming has been moving toward this finality for some time, and I am uneasy about it. It may be a place to turn down the page and close the book.

I have no doubt the professional agronomists and agricultural experts will all agree with the Brothers Allessio, and that every proof will be convincing. Butterfat will soar, poundage will increase, reclamation value will go up, quality control will be simplified, conversion will climb, and the farmer will have hours of leisure to sit by the television and peruse the trivial.

Yet I'm going to be a dissenting customer unimpressed by the back-patting of the professors and technicians with their inevitable clipboards, and no matter how conclusive the evidence, I'm going to believe otherwise. I happen to believe what this country needs most, right now, is another twenty or thirty million people who have driven cows to pasture and have enjoyed and profited from the experience. It has come to the point where some public character opens his head to contribute a thought, and you can tell right off that he never drove a cow to pasture, and wouldn't know how.

There was a time in our affairs when you could rally around a man, no matter how far he had gone, because you knew from the way he held himself, and the way he spoke, and the way he smiled, and the way he figured things out, that he had once been a boy who drove cows to pasture. And I see no way that bringing the pasture to the cows will ever contribute like qualities to the growing boy, or infuse him with extra senses and sensitivities.

It's been quite a while now that the trend has been leading up to zero pasturage. Gentle bossy has not lactated in an intimate and domestic fashion for some time. Milk control boards, market administrators, boards of health, and the arithmetic of economic survival have all contrived to whittle the thing down. The gentle family cow has given up her personalized position, and has become nothing more than a milk machine in a fabricating plant.

True, the figures show that we have more cows than ever before, but the figures also show that the tie-up that had two, three, four cows, maybe ten, is empty. Many a farmer found he could buy milk cheaper than he could grow it, or that government snooping wasn't worth the time. So while big dairy barns concentrate on production, many a farm boy grows up today without a cow and he doesn't get the useful exposure once so common.

The sun used to slant over the rim of our valley to find us already astir. No matter how hot the summer day would be, the grass now was cool and wet, and bare feet splashed in the dew on the way to the barn. The cows, of which we didn't milk more than one or two, would stand up when they heard us coming, and as we stepped through the open door and broke the spider webs of the night they would be stretching. A cow who has just risen from her downy couch likes to stretch her muscles just as anybody else does. And the pigs and hens and sheep would all be going through the same maneuver, getting ready for the breakfast ceremonies.

First would go a pailful of sour milk to the pigs, and this would quiet them down. Then a scattering of cracked grain to the hens, and a small dipper of grain to the cows that would be milked. We didn't know so much in those days about the factors of nutrimental ingestion, and the grain wasn't so much to feed the cow as it was to keep her quiet while she was milked. In the winter we grained them more, but in summer it was purely a diversion. Then, as the sun looked directly in the tie-up door and felt warm on those same bare feet, we'd straddle the little stool and strum-strum-strum on the bottom of the four-teen-quart milk pail. The strum would fade into a plushy drone, and then to a whisper as the froth formed on the top and the pail began to fill.

There was no putt-putt of a milking machine compressor, the clank and chrome of expensive equipment, or any assembly-line activity. We didn't have any trucks backing up with forty-quart cans whose covers needed jangling, or elaborate milk-room equipment. It was just a matter of sitting there quietly, to absorb a little sunshine through the feet, and to permit the eternal verities of the quiet life to seep through you in a kind of poetic osmosis until you had the cow dry.

We used to tidy up the barn work and leave the cows chewing on a morsel of millet while we went to the house and had breakfast, taking the pail of milk to the kitchen shelf. From the village, three miles away, we could hear the two toots on the 6:30 whistle at the mill. It was good to know we didn't have to respond to it.

After breakfast we drove the cows up to the pasture. Up the long lane through the orchard, where minister apples and red astrachans were waiting to be picked up; where raspberries riper and sweeter than yesterday's were hanging; where hazelnuts were filling out; and where ten thousand other things needed inspection. Maybe a hen partridge would have her brood out for a stroll, and perhaps a hawk or a fox would be interrupted by your arrival, because hawks and foxes like partridges, too. Almost always a brown snowshoe rabbit would thump his heels and sail over the wall.

On ahead the cows would march purposefully, intent on the day ahead. They'd stop to slat their heads at flies, and sometimes would need a touching up with the peeled willow wand that was the mace of this important ritual. You left the peeled wand by the bars at the gap, so it would be there at night for bringing the cows down again.

Of the four bars in the gap, only the top three were let down for the cows — they stepped over the bottom one. And they would step over and then fan out for the morning's grazing. You put the bars up, leaned the stick against the post, and leaned there a moment with your elbows on the top spruce pole. The pasture ran to about sixty acres, including the sugar bush, woodlot, swamp and ledges. Some of it had grass and was good for cows.

Not modern cows, of course; but modern cows

have nothing to do but give milk, and technology
has proved that they don't need a pasture to do that.
And if this is so, and it is, I foresee a dire and empty
future. Nobody, not even dairy farmers, will take
cows to pasture. The rich cultural experiences that
were always the side-values and profits are lost forever
to mankind.

WONDERS AREN'T ALWAYS BIG

One of the magazines prints an article
about the seven wonders of American engineering —
Panama Canal, Colorado River Aqueduct, Empire
State Building, Grand Coulee Dam, Hoover Dam,
Chicago's Sewage Disposal System, and the San Fran-
cisco–Oakland Bridge.

You will perceive that these are largish items; the
conclusion being that to be good, anything American
must be big. This is perhaps a fallacy, but it runs
through most of our national thought and may be
considered an inherent way of thinking. If it isn't big,
it isn't important, and if it isn't big it isn't American.

Well, you take this San Francisco bridge, and I am
ready to admit its engineers deserve applause, and I
don't wish to belittle it in any way. They had the

money, so they called in the talent, and they built it. Honestly, what's wonderful about that? Truth is, I can think of two bridges which interest me much more and which ought to be on any list of wonders. But neither of them is, and you never heard of them. One of them was "the longest single-span bridge in the world." I hope the conditioned American, seeing that claim and believing that nothing is big unless it is big, will envision something that goes on and on into perspective, and stretches across an endless sea. A tremendous continuity of bridge. Actually, this was a rather short bridge, and all it did was go across the Androscoggin River at Livermore Falls, here in Maine. The genius and the magnitude lie in the claim, rather than the bridge. The bridge was about the length of a bowling alley, and not much wider. You see, it isn't the longest bridge in the world, and it isn't even the longest span in the world. It was just the longest bridge ever made with one span. This is a wonderful thing, but when a magazine makes up a list of American engineering wonders, it goes off onto something like the San Francisco bridge, which is just another bridge.

I mentioned two. The second is "the only cast-iron bridge in the world." This one was at Bowdoinham, here in Maine again, and it went across the Cathance River. This wouldn't impress strangers, but it should

CATHANCE

Saunders

be pointed out that the Cathance (cat-hanse) River is one of the five streams making up the idyllic Merry-meeting Bay. The others are the Muddy, Abagadasset, Androscoggin and Kennebec. The Cathance is not a large stream, and in some places might be called a creek or a brook. In the history of the town of Bow-doinham, it came time to build a bridge over it, and the citizens duly considered the matter in town meeting.

A committee was appointed to investigate costs, and it conferred with the Boston Bridge Works, which has been engineer and consultant to eastern American bridge-building interests for lo, these many. The committee, at a subsequent meeting, reported its findings, and Bowdoinham found this project was going to cost a wad. At this point old Sam Reed asked to be recognized, and he told the town that he thought the price was high. Mr. Reed was an iron puddler, and he cast stoves in his little foundry alongside Cathance River. He made stoves and grates and or-namental ironwork, trivets and weathervanes, and he said he thought that he could cast a bridge cheaper than that. It would take a little time, but if the tax-payers wanted to save money and could wait, he was willing to try.

So Bowdoinham agreed to let Sam Reed make a bridge. First, he had to make the wooden patterns, and then he would cast a few pieces and put them on the bank of the river. Then he would make another pattern, and he would cast some more pieces. Time ran on, and piece by piece he cast the bridge. Then he had some rods come, and he cut bolts and tapped out nuts. One day all was ready, and the men got together and bolted up the bridge. It stood for over a hundred years, and was the only cast-iron bridge ever built.

I am sorry to have to report that the stupid commissioners of our Maine Highway Department did away with both these bridges, and replaced them with engineering triumphs that would please the editor of any modern American magazine. Neither of these bridges was gigantic, colossal, stupendous. The San Francisco bridge appeals to people because it cost $75,000,000, but the cast-iron bridge appealed to the taxpayers of Bowdoinham because it did not. The question comes on greatness.

Ah, there — I've often thought that the genius who invented the storm window did more for the American people than the man who dug the Panama Canal; that the set-over pung was a more magnificent contribution than the Empire State Building. But we live amongst people who think nothing is any good unless it is big, expensive, and terrific. Yet these are the seven engineering wonders of the modern world, and nobody asks what became of the seven wonders of the ancient world? They are all gone, except the pyramids — and they are old. Where will the seven engineering wonders of America be when they, too, are old? The Colossus of Rhodes is where? Will Sappho still smite her bloomin' lyre when the San Francisco bridge is legendary? I think so.

Or was it Homer?

Grand Coulee Dam weighs 22,000,000 tons. Look at it, and then come with me through the willows to the back acres, and I'll show you where a colony of beavers has built a dam lately which is quite a wonderful thing. It isn't very big, of course. Un-American, but clever.

SURREALISM IN WEATHERVANES

The inexorable retribution that propriety exacts from the malefactor has come home to roost; and the surrealist weathervane in Paderborn, Westfalia, is being replaced by one that works. Not always do we have this clear-cut chance to distinguish this from that, and it isn't surprising that our press has neglected the item. Wars and rumors of wars, and the occasional suggestion of peace, dominate our information, and our talented journalistic corps abroad has neglected this weathervane. Yet what is significant?

If we could adjust our perceptions to the thousandth of an inch, as we can our technocracy, we might even construe this weathervane as the biggest story of our time. It is, withal, a simple story. An ancient church, held dear in the hearts of the people, decided recently to add a weathervane to its utmost steeple. A normal, simple, logical, village desire. From the earliest times, long before the first church was built, man has lived with the wind. When he first crawled from his wickiup and stood erect to go forth and hunt his breakfast, he wet his finger and held it aloft to ascertain velocity and drift, so he could creep upwind to catch his prey. That wet finger was the first weathervane.

When architecture at last provided places where mechanical weathervanes might be permanently installed, a growing admiration for beauty and style prompted man to adorn his useful gimmick, and it is true that roosters, horses, cupid's darts and such-like artistry came into being; and he gilded them, wrought them o'er with brede, and so on. But for every gold-leaf fish and ship that pointed the wind there would also be the homemade wooden shingle on a barn or fence post. It was all the same, the first intent was to determine the flow of the wind; ornamentation was merely to adorn and had, itself, no function.

The weathervane became important in folklore, culture and society. Politicians who sat on a fence to see which way the cat would jump became "Weathervane Joes." Poetic images of inconstancy. George Flanders, who lived down the road here, once put up a milch cow, and under her the compass points read N, W, S and Ill. The east wind, you see, blows nobody good in these parts. But whatever was done with a vane, in waggishness or in art, kept true to the real purpose — a weathervane was to tell which way the wind blew.

I suppose civilization began to deteriorate, and as men drew away from their basics they became frivolous, and a condition of mind set in which, because we like to be polite, we called Surrealism. And after a time this, too, became accepted enough so the Surrealists were invited to design a weathervane for the ancient church in Paderborn. By this time there were definitions, and Surrealism in literature consisted of setting words down without logical sequence, and in art of giving weird, distorted forms to ordinary objects. What could be more ordinary than a weathervane? Where, in ordinariness, could a Surrealist be more open to distortion?

Now, so long as the Surrealist keeps his notions on

paper, there is no sound way to test the thing. Under our Constitution and By-Laws the poet and artist are protected, and each is his own authority. He creates, and it is public function to nod. This, I suppose, is why the correspondents kept one eye on the Saar and another on Geneva, and never noticed how the wind blew in Paderborn. You'd have thought all that was coming was another poem or another painting.

But whatever the weird, distorted form was, it neglected to respond to the vagaries of the Paderborn wind. The Surrealist weathervane was a dud. The parishioners, hereinafter referred to as the paying customers, would gaze aloft and behold the magnificent arrangement, and they had a twittering sense of beguilement, but they couldn't tell how things went with the wind. They had fulfilled the obligation of contract, but they were wetting their fingers again. It was a modern-day version of the old invisible cloth — the monarch who was conditioned by a sales talk until he believed he could see the fabric, and the clear vision of a child that pointed out the fraud. The Paderbornians had embraced Surrealism, but they tested it by the lay of the wind. It was found wanting.

I can hear the artist, or artisan, explaining his work! It's a new school, he says, with uninhibited expression. The meaning of the sweeping lines and the depth of perception complement the counterpoint and timbre — these are suggestive of the indomitable surge of jubilation and zeal. Here is suggested the hurtling vapors of the Atomic Age; here the quiet content of a cheerful disposition. A thousand aphorisms lie abstract in the delicate mobility of the moralization. The perversity of change is sweetened by the rigid axis, esoterically prognosticating a good day in Paderborn for drying the wash. But I can see the artist and the artisan, and the bright-eyed sycophants, explaining all this while the citizens of Paderborn stand to one side, look up at the Surrealist weathervane, and shake their heads.

Then the Paderbornians did a monumental thing. They took this Surrealist vane down, and they took it to an old-fashioned blacksmith, and they said, "Fix this!" They told him they wanted a plain, old-fashioned, reliable weathercock. Nothing fancy, nothing mystical, nothing suggestive. Just a rooster. Something that didn't burst into inferential neo-semantics, but would devote itself to indicating the wind.

We should all be grateful to the citizens of Paderborn, Westfalia, and the great lesson they have taught. Whencesoever it blows, I hope their wind is fair.

ONE WAY OR ANOTHER

A very fine letter is at hand in which certain opinions are expounded, and the gentleman concludes: "This should prove something one way or another." I'm inclined to favor this as a reasonable assumption; since earliest boyhood I have been aware that things are constantly proved to me, one way or another. I can tell you, for instance, of a happening that definitely did.

Long years ago here in town a pretty little custom started, and it kept up for quite a time. The townspeople used to gather on Thanksgiving Day morning for a chicken-pie breakfast, and a short session of prayer and hymn singing. Everybody went, and over the years they rotated the place amongst the several churches and lodge halls, and also had a different committee every year. When I was still small I was retained one year at the handsome emolument of twenty-five cents to pump the pipe organ in the Universalist Church, and at some point in the eight-verse version of No. 226 in the old book I decided I was earning every cent.

But it was a wonderful thing to see all the people coming in bright and early on the holiday, greeting each other and laughing. The meal was reasonable, tasty and fattening, and everybody was glad. And because the event had a new committee every year there was a certain effort at constant improvement, as the Pythian Sisters tried to outdo the Mizpah Class, and so on. But the general method remained about the same — chickens would be procured from some farmer, each lady would take one home and make a pie, and long before sun-up on Thanksgiving morning the pies would be collected.

The time therefore came when Mrs. Alonzo W. Sawyer was chairman of the committee. This is important. The Sawyer family was our leading family, both commercially and socially. When Mrs. Sawyer did something, it was done right. And everybody anticipated the biggest and best Thanksgiving breakfast in history. Mrs. Sawyer had announced her sub-committees, and all, and things looked in good shape.

Now, we had in town a certain fellow who did not travel in the same stratum as Mrs. Sawyer. He was an uncultured character whose career was not above reproach. Today a lot of people would be trying to rehabilitate him, and he would be the object of study by those who hold that society is rude to arrest anybody for anything. But in those days he was just Jim, let us say, and for the moment was free of encumbrances and obligations. He was on two overlapping and concurrent probations, and possibly he was touched by some slight feeling of contrition or penitence.

It is not for one of us to judge another, but a great many folks in town went to that trouble, and the illustrious citizen who was our barber, surveyor, real estate, insurance, notary public, horse-lawyer and magistrate had long since given up any illusions about reforming Jim by law and order. One time the judge was holding court and he had a fellow before him who had stolen some firewood. The judge gave him a little lecture and told him to stop being so lazy, that a man who couldn't cut his own firewood was the lowest of the low, and to get his gumption stirred and get to it. The courtroom was still ringing with this good advice when the constable brought in Jim, who had just been caught cutting firewood on the judge's woodlot. Most every town had a Jim in those days.

So Jim came and knocked on the front door of Mrs. Alonzo W. Sawyer one evening between supper and dishes, and Mrs. Sawyer was taken aback to find him standing there with his hat in his hand and on his face a warm, disarming smile that would melt the heart right out of you. Jim bowed from the waist and melodiously said, "Good evening!"

[146]

"Why, good evening, Jim," she said.

Jim said, "I was wondering, ma'am, if you've laid in the hens yet for the chicken-pie breakfast."

"No," she said. "We haven't."

"Well," said Jim, "I got to thinking, and you know, I'm kind of an old skunk, myself, and don't amount to much, and I thought I'd like to do my part. Everybody else in town turns to, and I never do nothin'. So, if you'd allow me to do it, I'd like to donate the chickens."

Mrs. Alonzo W. Sawyer said, "You'd like to do what?"

"Yes," said Jim. "I'd like to do it. You just say how many, and I'll bring 'em around all dressed and drawn, ready to go, and maybe it'll make up for some of the times I ain't been the fair-haired boy around town."

Mrs. Alonzo W. Sawyer said afterwards that the sweet spirit of charity was standing out on Jim like a barn on fire, and it made her all prickly-tingle to see the humble, wanting-to Jim make his offer to the cause. She brushed an unbidden tear from her eye and told Jim how many chickens they'd need.

Jim brought them. At the specified time he drove his wagon up with the birds all laid out on brown paper in big baskets, and the giblets in clean, white pails. The chickens were distributed to the women, the pies were baked, and on Thanksgiving morning they served the traditional breakfast to the gratified townspeople. Jim was given a free ticket, and he ate as hearty as anybody and had a good time. Nobody ever tasted any better chicken pies. Jim was commended on every hand.

The next morning Deputy Sheriff Charles M. Pulsifer arrested Jim for stealing Ken Babcock's poultry — which, as I said, goes to prove something, one way or another.

MEMORY TREADS

When I learned that President Eisenhower's farm at Gettysburg had a back stairway, I knew things were in good shape. All farms should have a back stairway, and I am perfectly aware of the fact that there are political nuances. Almost all our recent governors of Maine have used the back stairway. The treads are said to be thin in spots. Somebody would ask a governor what he thought about the likelihood of rain, and he would have to excuse himself and go down the back stairs to find out if his opinion was agreeable to the kitchen cabinet. Some of our governors weren't really sure-footed enough for this, so the kitchen cabinet would come right up into the office — but I'm not critical, I'm just showing that I know what a back staircase is.

The back staircase in our old farmhouse took off in the shed, and was a little steeper than the front staircase. At the top was the open shed attic, and a door that went into the house and the bedchambers. The shed attic was full of memorabilia and junk. The regular house stairs got most of the human coming and going, and the back stairs were the freightway.

I believe the high spot in the history of our back stairs was the occasion when my father, then a youth, started up with the parts to his high-wheeled bicycle just as his father, my grandfather, started down with all the flue pipes for the parlor stove. My father stepped on a box of spinning wheel spindles and his father stepped on a large and spirited yellow cat, after which the affair settled into a steady din. Aunt Prissy stuck her head out of the kitchen door and reminded that the baby was asleep, and my Uncle Cyrus (who was the baby) says he remembers it precisely and it is his first recollection. The jingling and the remarks tapered off after a time, but it was a noteworthy afternoon.

Back stairs were a place where the women put (a) things they would take up next time they went, or (b) things they would take down the next time they went. Because of their receding nature back stairs seem to remind women of whatnots and catch-alls. And this projection of things to do at sometime in the future never made allowances for the innocent citizen who chanced along and wasn't suspicious. Such innocent citizens would pass by blithely, catch their toes in an ice skate, bounce off a box of empty pickle jars, clutch at a firkin of Christmas ornaments, and descend via the sap buckets.

Even Cap'n Potter, the most dignified man ever to comport himself in our neighborhood, was no equal to back stairs. He fetched up one time with his head in a pail of eggs. They found him sitting on the shed floor, the pail on over his head, and the eggs streaming down like the ointment on Aaron's beard. Even Cap'n Potter got little sympathy, although as they said at the time he saw the yolk.

Well, the women never felt a man had any business on back stairs. He waived his rights when he went that way. No woman ever came right out and said, "Now, men, I have just put six cakepans, four skis, a bag of onions and sixteen jelly tumblers on the back steps!" This would not be playing the game. She would just put the things there and wait for the man to find them. When he had found them and lay a tattered wreck on the shed floor, she would come out from the kitchen and ask what in the world was making all that infernal racket? "Well, why don't you look where you're putting your big flat feet?" As I say, Cap'n Potter got little sympathy.

On rainy days we youngsters would go up those old back stairs to play with the things in the attic. We could find all manner of funny old hats and clothes in the boxes and trunks. We could outfit a real carpetbagger and his lady, or a rough old sea captain and his bride, and we found things like Benjamin Franklin's square spectacles and a thing to shoot the sun by. We didn't know how to shoot the sun, but it made crows up in the pasture look as big as roosters close to. And pictures — there were all sorts of pictures of ancestors and aunts.

With the rain thrumming on the roof the attic was an afternoon to remember a lifetime. Poke bonnets and white beaver hats! And Uncle Niah's old walking stick with a real dagger in the handle if you twisted it just right. Just why Uncle Niah ever had such a murderous weapon is a family mystery, for he was a deacon of the church, a quiet, perhaps sanctimonious, sort who was never over five miles from home in his whole eighty-nine years, and a tender man who always wept when it was time to veal the calves. The back stairs!

One year the squirrels filled the floor of the shed attic with acorns. They came out of the woods by way of a pine tree, bringing the acorns one at a time from the oak grove, and they'd leap to an apple tree and then to a pear, and finally jump to the ell roof. A knothole under the eaves gave them a way in, and they piled up about five bushels of acorns right in the middle of the floor.

Nobody knew this was going on, so there was no warning. Grandmother discovered the acorns. She came out of the back bedroom into the shed attic with a featherbed, and she walked right onto the pile of acorns. She immediately announced a distinct complaint which assembled everybody, and while we stood lined up on the back staircase, by height so all the heads were even, she skated around on the acorns for about fifteen minutes. She missed a few, but got the most of them. She executed many marvelous designs and proved she was an excellent skater, and then she fell on the featherbed and stopped skating.

Back stairways are a fine thing. I wouldn't be without one. They get better as they go along, and a family has time to improve on them. As long as we can have a president who knows about back stairways, the Republic is safe enough. He may have his head in a churn once in a while, but the Republic is all right.

MOONS AND SUITORS

When the Age of Fission finally got around to launching its first satellite, the American Rocket Society retained lawyers to look into the grave question of who owns outer space, anyway. Here was a device, cunningly contrived, which was to burst from the atmosphere and proceed into the periphery and dangle, and this would raise the ticklish question of title and equity. Astronomers on other planets might stand on their respective peaks of Darien and view our rockets with wild surmise, but lil ol' homo sapiens would have writin's from the registrar of deeds.

As a citizen conversant with much, I had a certain kind of misgiving about our rocketry. In general, I think the Space Age enjoyed the confidence of the public to a degree that never prevailed before. They laughed at Ben Franklin when he flew a kite, and at Bob Fulton when he steamed up his boat. But nobody ever laughed at nuclear physicists and astronauts — the premise was accepted and everybody expected them to be right. In recollection, it occurs to me that I never doubted that they would put a vehicle in orbit, or open the secrets of interstellar traffic.

But what I did doubt, and the thing that gave me misgivings, was the American Way when it comes to implements, devices and gadgets. I have had too much trouble with refrigerators, furnaces, washing machines and other domestic appliances. I would not want to be up there in an American-made satellite and have to wait while a repairman comes and installs a new washer on the main bearing. America is the nation where everybody sells wonderful new machines, but nobody cares a hoot about keeping them going or fixing them when they break. I was leery of the long-term chances of rockets made in the U.S.A.

I felt it was going to be very poor advertising for us when we got a moon-machine up there, and all the other nations and all the other planets could look and see "Pat. Pending, U.S.A." painted on the tail, and there it floated for six months with a flooded carburetor while the local distributor got in touch with the home office and put a trouble-shooter on the job.

I can report factually that it takes three months with a simple dishwashing machine that sits under a kitchen shelf, and then only after a snappy letter to the main plant. The trouble was with the rubber gasket that seals the front and keeps the machine from leaking on the floor. With a furnace important enough to use full-color advertising in the major magazines, it took from August 26 to December 7, inclusive, and the man came four times — getting paid for each time, of course.

Around home, where we understand the American System, this isn't too important, and we've learned to live with it. We pay our money for a dishwashing machine, and then when it blows a gasket we leave it sitting there under the shelf and wash dishes by hand until somebody gets around to fixing it. *Ça va.* But to put this kind of technology on display to the ends of infinity where whole galaxies can watch us seems to me to be a kind of national folly, and I wouldn't suppose it would do our economy any good.

And, it's true that we are up against a pretty stiff competition. I have observed that the original moon is fairly efficiently constructed, and seems to be working now as well as it did when it was first brought to my attention. I can't see but it keeps to its course pretty well, and that it waxes and wanes with as much enthusiasm as ever. Just the other night I rolled over in bed and chanced to look through the window at the moon, and I was struck by the fact that it shines now, after all these years, just as good as a new one. It doesn't show any wear and tear.

You'll find it's kind of amusing to wonder who owns the moon. There she was humping along all unconcerned, and men down on Earth were scanning the big lawbooks to see where possession is defined. The wild surmise bows to due process of law. Everything is ready to touch off a few fuses, but a legal opinion isn't in yet.

There have been a few times when I felt, honestly and sincerely, that the moon and stars were mine. Many a pleasant evening I have wandered along by myself, feeling maybe like something turning on an axis and pursuing an orbit, and I have had a possessive notion that a whole universe of property belonged to me. Some evenings I leave them far and indistinct, and some evenings I have them right down so I could, if I wanted to, climb into an apple tree and pick them.

I suppose, now that the Beyond has been breached, somebody will come around some day and take all these things away from me. This will be too bad, because somewhere in silly little Man there has always been an earthbound conceit — magic casements opening on the foam. Nightingales, stars, southerly winds, and such. Now the mortgage is being foreclosed, and star by star and nightingale by nightingale we can expect the little signs to go up: "Keep Off, Private Property." I don't have any signed paper in the black tin box to exhibit in court, so from now on the moon is in probate.

But there is an equity there, and I'm just waiting

for that night when Chaste Diana hunts across my sky, and suddenly she is obscured by an American Made satellite — one with a weak picture tube, a peeling paint job, and a cracked muffler. I won't need any lawyer to tell you, then, which is mine.

WHEELS AND MORNING GLORIES

Like pussy cats, every subject has its pros and cons, and I'm wondering how we stand, percentagewise, on wagon wheels. When I socialize and travel hence, I'm surprised to find so many people use the lowly wagon wheel as an emblem of beauty and a joy forever by working them into the front lawns of America. It seems to me some wheelwright, his traditional trade long gone, could make a fortune by turning out wheels for suburban decorations — wheels that never supported a load, will never turn, supporting mailboxes and morning glories.

Personally, I don't care much for the wheel as an adornment of the landscape. I have a number of old wheels around here, what the auction bills call the accumulation of a lifetime, and it never occurred to me to set them up in public view as an enhancement of the periphery. I've two real oxcart wheels behind the barn, with buttonwood hubs, and they were once cast aside in reckless abandon by some progenitor who was glad to be shut of them. If somebody should stop by and offer me twenty-five dollars apiece I would even help him load them.

Not long ago I saw a spanking new motel, dedicated to the high-speed purposes of the throughway trade, and the landscaping included a fine wagon wheel by each cubicle door. It looked like a wide front of architectural mobility, ready to roll like a fire engine or a Greek phalanx, crushing all in its path. I would not like to sleep there. I would worry about being ridden away in the night like a runaway wagon, possibly ending up in a strange town in my night clothes.

I am, however, willing to believe that some minds find the wheel a lovely design. The circular shape may be symbolic of universal beneficence, encompassing totality, the spoked segments suggesting hope, frugality, perseverance, thrift, cleanliness, and the democratic process. The hub would represent the individual guest, equidistant from his obligations and well adjusted socially. The motel, I might add, was called Wagon Wheels.

I assume that these countless opportunities for philosophic deductions, and the suggestion of geometric morality, are the reasons so many people offer the wheel by the front door. Detached from its parent stem to become a static emblem of esoteric complexities, it pleases the roving eye and looks nice. My trouble is that I am an old-timer, and I look upon the wheel with aging eyes. I can remember when a wheel was a wheel, and I am aware of many things the new suburbanite wots not of.

I have, for example, one large memory of greasing the buggy wheels Sunday morning. It should have been done Saturday but it wasn't, and Monday would be too late — Grandmother allowed that she had ridden to town on screeching, howling, bone-dry axles for the last time, that lubrication was in order, and that there was no need of announcing your progress toward sabbath services from three miles up the road. In those happy times grease was not merely a silencing agent, but it gained that effect and was not altogether necessary as a lubricant. It did make the wheels turn more easily for the horse, but no farm cart ever caught fire because it wasn't greased. We didn't go that fast. So we didn't bother much until Grandmother made us.

A new generation that rides on a "film of oil" wouldn't know about gudgeons. A gudgeon is a pivot or journal, that part of the axle on which a wheel turns. Every farm had a pail of gudgeon grease in the shed, with a little wooden paddle for applying it, and because of the infrequent use the grease would cake over on the top and look like a defunct custard. So after Grandmother had reminded us all week to grease the gudgeons and we hadn't done it, she raised the question Sunday morning, "Did you grease up?" So we got out the wagon jack and the pail of grease, and we greased up Sunday morning.

The wagon jack was nowhere near so sophisticated as today's bumper lifters; it had two positions, up and down. It worked like a bent-back elbow, and lifted the wagon just high enough to slip off a wheel. We had a wagon wrench that started the big nuts, and there were left-hand nuts on one side and right-hand on the other. The direction kept the nuts on — if you backed a wagon too far those nuts would come off and you were in a fix. Some modern automobiles still use left-hand nuts, and they can be a surprise to an uninformed mechanic, but on a wagon they were standard.

So we greased the buggy and pleased Grandmother. There wasn't a squeak as we rode to town. The Silent Sunday, we called it. But those of us who hurriedly went out and applied the grease in the last few moments before departure, with the distant first bell sounding across the valley, wore evidence to meeting. Sunday suits and gudgeon grease are close friends. Grandmother rubbed our clothes with lard and naphtha all week, and fretted some at the general intelligence of her family.

A dished wheel is another memory. Age would prompt a wheel to lose its grip on the hub, and for a time the wheel would ride all right, but it had a jaunty, care-not expression. Then all at once it would collapse and let you down. Some farmers rode on dished wheels for years, sitting on the seat with an expression of momentary expectancy, and imagining that every rock in the road would be the one.

The rimwracked wheel gave us a phrase. The spokes would fret loose in the rim, wearing their mortises larger, and there would be a chattering and chowdering as you went along. If you went to the wheelwright soon enough he could save things, but hardly anybody ever did. Once in a while you'll hear somebody say such-and-such is rimwracked, but it's hardly ever a wheel any more.

So, the world is full of happy homeowners with antique wheels adorning their lives, but they wouldn't know a gudgeon or a wagon jack if they saw one. Unimportant, but perhaps interesting.

RAMRODDING vs. RUMINATION

Finding a mess of chimney swifts had moved into his fireplace flue, my friend Pat Sawyer took steps to remove them. At first he didn't know just how to go about this, but as he began he was surrounded by experts. It was another friend, Leon Bard, who said once that nobody needs to know anything any more. All he has to do is start a job, and immediately a congregation of onlookers will tell him how. This is what happened with Pat — he had all sorts of advice from everybody.

Anyway, during this effort to dislodge the swifts, one poor little bird became so terrified that he dropped down on the hearth of Pat's living-room fireplace, and just hunched up there a-quiver. Pat picked him up, stroked his feathers, carried him outdoors, held him aloft in the palm of his hand for a takeoff, and said, "Fly away in peace, my fine feathered friend!"

Then the swift flew back into the chimney.

Behold how potent runs the moral of said tale! A great many times, for us, the swift flies back into the chimney, and with much labor and to-do we assault the daily chore, only to find the evensong upon us just about as it was yesterday at this time. I think letters to the editor. I keep seeing swifts flying back into chimneys.

Here is a letter written by a professor of electrical engineering at a prominent and well-respected western university, and he writes a letter to the editor saying, "It was difficult for me to guess whether the article was intended as humor, or if the author was serious."

It is a wonderful thing to focus on a professor of electrical engineering while he sits with head in hand, his brows knit, pondering on a good guess. I would like to see him wet a finger and go down in my cellar and make a shrewd guess about what circuit is hot, and stick his finger in a few sockets. I have an idea his contributions to culture seek to dissuade the student electrician from making this kind of a guess — but now the professor sits in his study and can't tell humor from what we assume is non-humor. I haven't had to deal with professors now for quite a good time, but I remember it was mighty hard to maintain an A grade by guesswork. This professor writes on, "In either case, the interpretation of the article by the public could be unfortunate."

Probably the most unfortunate possibility in this whole exchange lies in the way our great modern public accepts titles and position as a basis of proof. Like a professor. The word professor, applied to a man, leads many people to presume that he has qualifications for knowing, not guessing, and that when he opens his mouth to teach something the flow of words is measured and precise. This creates a loaded kind of debate in which the intellectual merit of the cause is smothered by the weight of the personality who advances an opinion. If you are a professor, your thoughts are worthy willy-nilly, and a non-professor who dares to dispute is an upstart. The swift goes back in the chimney, sort of.

Here is another letter to the editor from the executive secretary of a national turnpike association. His theme is that an editorial dealing with turnpike affairs was overly gratuitous. Nobody, he thinks, has a right to express himself about turnpikes unless he is an authority on the subject, and the only way you can become an authority on turnpikes is to be elected secretary of a national turnpike association. It is a kind of cloture rule, in which everybody is demoted to an amateur unless he happens to agree with the rules set up beforehand. Everybody else is wrong. It is intellectually illegal to observe that the bird is back in the flue.

Every once in a while the editor is deluged by letters pro and con about the fluoridation of public water supplies, and those in favor limit the discussion to the noble question of dental benefits. I have read these communications with great interest for many years, and the ardent opposition to fluoridation is always interpreted by the pros as a mean disposition toward little children with teeth, and a hatred of progress. It is clearly a snob argument, intended to shame the antis into silence.

Yet I have never seen any fluoridationist admit in his correspondence that there is any crass commercial tinge to the idea — which is something every fluoridationist knows, and knows precisely and in detail. Whenever a community begins to ponder fluoridation, the salesmen show up. They have a deliberate and extremely clever sales pitch, and they beset the officials until the town makes its decision. They sell the chemicals, the equipment, and the instructions. After you have heard one talk, you realize that not once in the whole conversation did he say anything about teeth. The nobility of the cause, as expounded in the press and in the town meeting, is not the nub of the matter, at all. An expert is a man who has something to sell.

Of course, people of prominence, position and experience may be right. But it would be nice if they would convince us fairly, and not hush us up by saying, "Look, I'm the expert, you have no right to question me!" Particularly if they are just guessing.

You can load a gun with a ramrod, but the process of rumination takes a little chewing.

I have no idea what Pat Sawyer should have done with his little swift, but off and on I shall try to give the matter some thought.

NAILING THE HORSESHOE NOTION

The custom of attributing salutary properties to a "charm" found some expression around the State of Maine in the horseshoe. The reason for attributing good luck to a horseshoe must be long lost in pre-Maine times, and I've certainly never heard anybody try to explain it. Most of our growing up in this area was reasonably sensible and practical, and we were taught to deplore frivolous thinking. Unequivocally, we were taught that reliance on good luck tokens was utter folly, but almost everybody had a horseshoe tacked up over a shed door.

Indeed, I can remember specifically having all this explained to me point-blank. Grandmother said that knocking on wood to invalidate a conversational exposure ("I never had a cake fall on me yet"— knock-knock) was plain foolishness. She hooted at all the folklore superstitions as they came up, carefully making all the children aware that they were nonsense. Spilling salt, stepping on cracks, going under a ladder, dropping a fork — intelligent people would be unconcerned. But Grandmother always touched wood, we noticed.

I can remember, too, how Grandfather told me a horseshoe should always be nailed up with the open part at the top, like a cup, else the good fortune inherent would naturally spill out and be wasted. This seemed to me to be a refinement, an inference on an inference and he, too, assured me the whole thing was absurd anyway.

When our big barn was built in 1919 one of the carpenters, Bert Hunnewell, got a horseshoe to nail over the grainroom door. He did it with all the seriousness in the world, although Bert didn't have a superstitious shred in his whole body. It was a gesture like to dropping a coin in a new well, or stepping a ship's mast on a silver coin. Bert did it because it was something generally done. That horseshoe fell off last summer, and I smiled about old Bert as I went and got a hammer and nailed it back. I nailed it well, and went inside the barn and headed the nails over, because I don't want it to fall off again — it might hit somebody. I put the open end up.

Historically, I suppose evidence could be mustered to show that a horseshoe wasn't too lucky for horses. Our last one was dated 1934. It was about the time

Mr. Craig stopped blacksmithing. Mr. Craig had a lot of horseshoes, but his business declined. But there had been many horses on our acres since oxen days (indeed, the two types of draft animals overlapped, and some of the oxen got shod, too), and I suppose many long years will pass before the last of the cast shoes will be found and used as lucky pieces.

I picked one up on the cutterbar of the mower, and it cost me seventy-eight dollars for repairs. I was lucky it didn't cost more. But I did put the rusty old shoe over a limb on a tree by the meadow, and after haying I brought it up and nailed it to the wall of the barn. I did this according to an old superstition I made up by myself, that a horseshoe nailed to a barn isn't going to foul up a cutterbar again.

Horses dropped old shoes wherever the nails gave out, and I find them with equal random. I was digging out to repair the stonework around the spring and threw out a rust-encrusted shoe which was certainly there since 1828, because that's when the spring was last dug around. I found one where I was fixing some pansies by the barn, and another when I transplanted some raspberries out back. Once I snagged one right over the point of the plowshare when I was breaking some sodground, and it fetched the rigging up so the wheels on the tractor spun and I was almost pitched off. I was lucky I was in a low speed gear.

So, speaking of horseshoes, I went the other day to a wholesale iron and steel establishment to get me some strap iron to brace some shelves I was putting up in the shop. I can get pieces chopped off into eighteen-inch lengths, and when I bore quarter-inch holes in them and bend them in the vise I get shelf brackets at a fraction of the going cost, and I am in favor of that.

I told the man what I wanted, and while he was hunting it down I wandered through the warehouse and looked at the bridge girders, cement reinforcements, structural beams, and all the other magnificent fabrications of modern engineering that were piled all over the place. Trucks and dollies were coming and going, and business was good. They had cranes and hoists, and I thought it was something of an imposition to ask them to pause in the pursuit of prosperity and whack me up a mere five dollars worth of iron. But you can't always tell.

I stepped through a door into another shed, and there was a man all by himself piling over a vast quantity of horseshoes. These were new horseshoes, in that they had never been attached to a horse. They were piled by sizes and weight, and the man was counting them. He would count, and then write a figure on a clipboard, and then count some more.

It was a jingling and jangling job, and since he couldn't talk while counting I had a difficult time setting up a straightforward conversation, but he could see that I was interested and after a moment he paused in his inventory. He told me that these horseshoes had been prepared many years ago on the assumption that horses were here to stay. These were stock shoes, to be supplied wholesale to farriers in the hinterland. Blacksmiths bought by sizes and weight, by the gross, and didn't need to manufacture from scratch. They needed only to make such changes as would fit the hoof. Calks and bars came separate, and could be attached on the forge as needed.

Thus the end of the horse era found this warehouse well stocked, and based on current demand they had enough stock shoes on hand to last about ten million years. True, the man said with some optimism, they did sell some now and then, and just the other day a blacksmith in a lumber camp in Piscataquis County had sent in a large order for ten pairs. But the movement, he indicated, was not brisk.

I asked him if he advanced the price as steel moved up, but he said no — they could still quote a 1910 price with trade discounts. He said he doubted if they would ever recover full capital investment, but as an accommodation item they wouldn't close them out. I suggested the horseshoe hadn't exactly been a lucky item, had it, and he laughed a good bit at that and said no, he guessed not, and he went back to counting.

TOO MUCH PICKLE JUICE, AND POOF!

A gentleman with mercenary motives and a lack of finer discernment is advertising a make-your-own-antiques kit, complete with printed instructions and nail holes indicated. This should be deplored. It is not as easy as that to make antiques. To postulate that every Tom, Dick and Harry can turn out top-grade early artifacts the same as he'd glue plastic airplane models together is absurd. That would glut the market with spurious items, the work of amateurs, easily detected, and it would depress the market for authentic antiques turned out lovingly by masters of the craft.

It takes a love of line and design, an understanding of art and artistry, and a fine sense of feel to make a really good antique these days.

I've made a great many antiques in my day, and although I have enjoyed some attention for it, I'm not really that good at it. But the smallish things I have turned out satisfy me enough so I feel qualified to speak. Actually, I got my start through a bargain in boots. I was in the country store upstate and the man showed me a pair of cowhide boots that were pegged in his grandfather's time. They were in reasonable condition, but needing some neatsfoot oil, and I made him a small offer which he accepted. He asked me what I planned to do with them, and I said I planned to wear them.

I wore them one day around the farm, and at night I couldn't get them off. Cowhide boots were like that. Friends and relatives gathered to straddle my foot, while I pushed with the other from behind, but nothing happened. I had to make a bootjack before I could go to bed. We used to have bootjacks around the farm years ago, and I remembered what one looks like.

After I got my boots off I bored a hole in the bootjack and hung it on a peg in the shed, and the next summer a transient saw it and said he would give me a dollar if he might have it. I couldn't think of a single reason why I should disappoint him, so he took it home to New Jersey where he tells people how he found it hanging on a peg in a barn up in Maine. He uses it for a doorstop, and I have been in the bootjack business ever since. I've made a good many since then, and the price now is two-fifty. I enjoy making people happy in this small way, and I like to think how folks display my bootjacks with pride.

This man tells his customers how to "age" antiques. He advocates rubbing with a chain, and letting the children bang things around. This is the basest of frauds. It will never do an authentic job. A real antique, made by a sensitive workman, is more artfully aged, and there is absolutely no short cut to perfection. The best way is to dip in ammonia and rub with wet hardwood ashes, molasses, pickle juice and butter. A small dash of red ochre in the butter makes a finish that won't rub off when the customer restores the finish.

If a man is really good at it, he can make modern antiques that are better than real ones. Too many antiques have only age to recommend them. I learned this as a boy. My mother had a parlor set that was "handed down" to her. It was a love seat and two chairs. They were up in the pigeon loft of the barn, and although they were old enough they were not from our family. Somebody had bought them cheap at an auction, and because they weren't comfortable they got put up in the barn. My father climbed up through the hole one day and handed these antiques down to my mother. She stood on the barn floor and reached up and took them when he handed them down. Then they had them redone, and when they were put in the front room we found a nail keg was better to sit on. This was a good lesson to me, and when I make antiques I try to fashion them so they are comfortable as well as old.

I made a lovely baroque, or Restoration, table once, using a hackmatack stump. I cut it so the roots formed the pedestal and the trunk supported the ornately carved top. I don't carve too well, because I have a dull knife, but I can whack around with an ax and make things look old. This table has attracted a lot of attention in its time, and if you count the rings in the pedestal you'll see that it is over a hundred and fifty years old.

But you can't, you see, just buy a ready-made kit and start an antique business. You've got to learn it step by step, and put your love into it, and by trial and error master the intricacies. It takes a year or two of patient application. It isn't just a matter of hitting a board with a hammer — you've got to know where to hit, and which hammer to use. It takes restraint, too — many a promising antique has been spoiled by over-zeal and injudicious enthusiasm. Just a bit too much pickle juice, and poof!

I think it would be wise to leave the making of antiques to those who specialize in it. Let people cut their own hair, or paint the ceilings in their own homes and make model ships. The great popularity of how-to-do-it and make-it-yourself needs to recognize that antiques are not just something else. They take at least a little time, and some talent.

NO FRINGE BENEFITS

The inexorable flight of unyielding time having caught up with me again, I went down the other day to have my hair pruned, and catch up with affairs. Richie welcomed me, and exercised his clippers while he filled me in, and when it came to the point where he always used to sweep my neck off with a long-spilled brush he came at me, instead, with a wadded-up towel and dusted me most inadequately.

I asked him if he'd lost his brush.

"No," he said. "Can't use it any more. New law. Unsanitary."

I realize, of course, that Maine is often far behind the politer trends, and that benefits and boons already firmly established in more enlightened places find us belatedly. Probably the long-spilled barber's brush made its last stand here.

I told Richie I didn't like the new rule, that my neck had long been conditioned to periodical sweepings, and it certainly wouldn't prove any more unsanitary now than it had the last time, and that I wasn't going to feel fully barbered without that finishing touch, sanitary or unsanitary.

Then I told Richie about the fellow from Schenectady who got his hair cut at Jim Ridley's barber shop in Township Three East, Range Four, back when things really were unsanitary and uncouth. Twp. 3E4 is really just a surveyor's arbitrary mark on a map, and Jim Ridley was the blacksmith for a lumbering operation run by King Midas Goodhue, one of the old-timers who wasn't much on style and sanitation, but knew how to make money.

King had a tramway built over Kajeemis Bog, and business was brisk. In his blacksmith shop, Jim had a Micmac boy to pump the bellows. He wasn't exactly a college man, and hadn't become what modern standards would call civilized, but he could pump a bellows fine. He never had had his hair cut, and this added a wild touch to the scene and indicated that the action took place outside the city limits.

So one rainy day Jim put the Micmac boy on the anvil and pared his locks with the horse clippers, and made a fairly decent-looking fellow of him. Seldom had anybody shown such concern for the boy, and he was grateful. He waited on Jim hand and foot after that, and around the logging operation he would doff his toque to choppers and sawyers, showing them what a nice job Jim had done.

Well, you see, a haircut in the Maine woods was unknown in those days. You came to work in September with your head cut like a honeydew melon, and you went out in May with the ingredients of a mattress. The first and last thing a woodsman did in town was to have his hair cut. And the sudden discovery that haircuts were available in camp brought everybody clamoring to Jim. "I ain't no barber," said Jim. But the pressure was too great, and Jim became a barber. He would cut hair when the smithing slacked off, and everybody was pleased — including old Midas Goodhue, who noticed that the men were more cheerful when clipped and accordingly produced more logs.

So, this man came from Schenectady that year. He was an electrical engineer, and his company thought they might be able to sell an electric locomotive to Midas Goodhue for his tramway. I don't know what the people in Schenectady think a tramway is, but this fellow showed up, and after he found out his mistake he stayed around a while, eating hearty and playing cribbage, and the boys liked him so it was all right.

Then Miss Cornish, the schoolteacher down at the Five Mile Camp of the Bigelow Industries, heard that this electrical engineer was in, and she sent up a note that she'd like to have him speak to her pupils some afternoon, probably because nobody at Five Mile had ever seen an electrical engineer, and he could perhaps explain what an electric locomotive was supposed to do on a tramway. This sounded to the man from Schenectady like a fairly good offer, so he came into Jim's blacksmith shop the next day and said he wanted a shave and a haircut, as he was booked for an academic lecture down at Five Mile.

So Jim threw a horse blanket over the anvil, and perched the fellow astride it, and went to work. He had some water hot in a pail on the forge, and he brought in a bar of Sunny Monday soap from the washstand in the dingle. He worked the horse clippers around the ears, and did the trimming with some tinsnips. He wrapped an oats bag around the fellow's neck, lathered him up good, and shaved him with a double-bitted Snow & Neally chopping ax. The whole performance took nearly four minutes, and now he was sweeping off the back of the fellow's neck with an ancient device now long forgotten, and probably never used but this once in the trade of barbering — it was a second-hand horse's tail attached to a handle. This brush was native to all well-conducted farrier shops, was handy a hundred times a day, and turned out to be a wonderful neck-sweeper too.

Then Jim doused his customer with the traditional toilet talcum which every woodsman believed, in the old days, was an unfailing disinfectant, insecticide and deodorant, all in one. The Maine woods would never have been logged off without talcum powder. And when Jim got the fellow powdered he whisked the grain bag from his neck, stood back and shouted "Next!" and they trotted in a Percheron gelding with a loose shoe.

Oh, I don't mean to condone these antique crudities, and maybe I'm not trying to make a point either. But the man from Schenectady said it was by far the best shave and haircut he ever had, and since Jim wouldn't let him pay, being a guest in camp, he tipped Jim a ten-dollar bill, and Jim said he'd just as soon have that as money.

But don't you think it's somewhat amusing that a state with this dainty idyll in its rough wilderness history should now, after all these years, become so neat — so nasty neat — that the barber's long-spilled brush has been outlawed as a barbaric device, unclean and deplorable, and I can no longer get my neck swept at Richie's?

THE MISSING TWO OUNCES

    After winding endlessly through the maze of our local supermarket for what I thought was longer than enough, I thrust my head into the air and let out a yell that suggested I was in dire straits and would appreciate assistance. If somebody concluded a band of heathen brigands had me by the throat it would be all right. I was between the spaghetti and the paper napkins, and my blood-curdling cry bounced around amongst the inventory so you wouldn't believe it.

I always shall and I always have. I resent being made to wait on myself when I go into a man's place of business to spend my money with him. I think he is rude, unkind, and economically unwise to put me to this trouble to find the goods that he wants to sell. And I don't like it when I can't find the vanilla and there is nobody around to tell me where it is.

So my yelp brought the owner, bearing in one hand a numbering machine with which he puts prices on cans, and yanking with the other at a revolver which didn't seem to want to come out of his hip pocket under the apron. He looked fully expectant of the worst, which is what I intended, and I grabbed him by his front and shook him and said, "Where are the mixed nuts?"

"Oh, it's you," he said, and he led me around a couple of corners, down an aisle of dogfood and cake mixes, past the puddings and frozen foods, and pointed at the mixed nuts between the peanut butter and the magazines.

"Give me two pounds," I said.

He gestured indifferently toward the shelf in the manner of one who has long since given up manual labor as an instrument of policy, and would have walked away if I had not, in a low, snarling, evil and ugly voice, articulated menacingly, "Give me two pounds!" I was just as mean as I could be. At the same time I half-gestured that I would yank out a bottom can and flood his store with tinned peaches and strained baby foods, so he decided to be tractable and reached me two packages of mixed nuts.

I will ask the court to observe particularly my selection of words. I asked for two *pounds*, and he handed me two *packages*. When I got home I found that each package said, in small print obscurely bestowed, NET WEIGHT: 14 OUNCES.

We discussed this in great terms of humanitarian constants for a time at home, and we don't think it is very nice. In the placards and advertising, my neighborhood grocer is supposed to be a kindly sort who stands for probity and looks after my interests with unyielding zeal. Food is the best bargain for our dollars, and the grocer is a good man. True, he doesn't package many of the things himself, and the mixed nuts are weighed before they come to him. But somebody, somewhere, in the chain of handling, made this modern decision about how much a pound of mixed nuts shall weigh.

It wouldn't cost a bit more, when preparing that package, to print NET WEIGHT: 14 OUNCES in big type than it does to print it in light diamond size, so we do have the right to raise the nasty question of why they obscure this information. It could just as well be erected in a good black 48-point boldface, and we consequently have the right to be suspicious of motives. Why does my kindly grocer try to fool me?

Afterwards, we looked at a number of packaged items from our cupboard, and we found that the pound is no longer in common use. Not in the stores. At home, of course, we jot down the grocery list and say a pound of this and a pound of that. But we come home with fourteen ounces of this and that. Raisins are in a pound package that weighs fourteen ounces. A pint can of milk has thirteen ounces liquid, fourteen and a half avoirdupois. Macaroni and spaghetti, for some reason, still sell at sixteen ounces to the pound, but are two of the few remaining honest-weight foods.

I found myself thinking, as so often happens, about the old ways and the new. We used to have a similar way of handling cordwood. The way wood grows, it isn't easy to pile it uniformly. Here in Maine the legislature took that fact into account when it defined a cord of wood — "allowance" is made for crooked limbs and knots. Five different people could pile a cord of wood and have five different quantities. Buyer and seller easily dispute over the measure. Every town had a public official known as the scaler who could be called in to protect the customer, but even that was no sure answer. In effect, buying stovewood was a working combination of caveat emptor and implied warranty. You couldn't go by weight, because some wood was dry and some wasn't. So we worked out a solution, which was to stop going by the "cord" and to deal in a "load." The size of the load depended on the size of the cart. Sometimes the load was a "jag," which is all you can haul without having any slide off. By lexicographer's extension the word today applies to something very different from wood, but that's what it meant.

But nobody ever sold a jag for a cord, or insisted that a load was one hundred twenty eight cubic feet. "This ain't a cord, you understand — just a load!"

was the wood dealer's constant reminder. It takes a modern grocer to show us just how honest the old folks were. Why didn't my grocer say to me, "Look, this isn't really a pound — it's just a package," and live up to the placards and advertising? I don't know, and it bothers me. Besides making me do his store-keeper work for him, and hunt around for anything I need, he puts out fourteen-ounce pounds with the implication that I'm too stupid to know the difference. I think what we need are a lot more people to stand in behind the cookies and spices and yell once in a while.

A MUSICAL SCROOGE?

When Scrooge made his television debut in a musical, I was able to restrain myself, and I did not watch. I didn't have to see it, because I had already imagined a musical Scrooge many times over, and after I had seen the television musical of Heidi I didn't feel the need of any more television musicals. I heard about it several weeks before Christmas when I was listening to a hockey game. On radio. The men were putting a new top on the ice between periods, and the announcer said he would now play one of the songs in the forthcoming television presentation of Scrooge. Then a lady sang a song that told me there is a Santy Claus, even though perhaps I don't see him. I was hoping she would add, "Yes, Virginia," but she didn't.

As I say, this was several weeks before Christmas, so I had some time to wonder where, in the staging of Scrooge, it would be most appropriate to insert a lady vocalist to substantiate the persistent rumors about Santy. I didn't decide, really, but the rumination revamped my grumpy old notions, and I could see many ways that the Scrooge story could be improved.

When you think about it, you'll have to agree that the old curmudgeon didn't dance quite as much as he ought, and that the morality of the story needs the pepping up of a few catchy tunes. A hot orchestration would certainly improve the hard-hitting traditionalism of the Lionel Barrymore rendition — which it seems to me has the disadvantage of being too much like Dickens. It lacks glitter and glamor, and everybody knows that what the Christmas story needs is some glitter and glamor.

So, although I didn't watch this improvement I thought out several possible ways to do Scrooge as a musical, and I think my best one is like this:

Mr. Jimmy Durante, in white tie and tails, wearing a beret and sneakers, is shown coming out of the Chase Manhattan Bank, main office, where he is vice president in charge of the questions on the big *Bonanza Buster* quiz show, sponsored on the network by this institution. Comely danseuses in holly-trimmed tights, wearing Brink Express caps, surround him (for safety), and as they dance he sings the first song. It is called "Christmas in Flatbush," and a portion goes like this:

> *My money's lent at ten per cent,*
> *I thrive on the improvident;*
> *At Christmas time I sue for rent,*
> *And that's the way my time is spent;*
> > *Fol de riddle, etc.*

The dance by the young ladies turns out to be a routine to deck the Yule tree, which they do with cashier's checks for a million dollars each.

It develops, you see, that Mr. Durante, or Scrooge, has repented of his penurious and skinflint ways, and has decided to give away, tonight, the entire assets of the bank to the contestant who can sing "Deck the Halls with Boughs of Holly" backwards while suspended by his heels over a tank of ice water. This is that part where the announcer laughs and shouts, "Aren't People Funny!"

The scene now shifts to the television studio where contestants are arriving to be rehearsed. Bob Cratchit, the elbows out of his seersucker suit, is just off the street, chattering from the cold and a pitiful sight. From his wan condition you can see that it has been a long time since he had any roast beef and Yorkshire pudding, but the make-up man is cutting his hair and making him pretty because the alternate sponsor is Apex Dandruff Shampoo and Scalp-Tone Inc. But as Bob walks out and is shown the chalk mark where he must stand, you can see that he is not downhearted. He is joyful with thoughts of the Holiday, and the prospect of winning a vast sum tonight to brighten his Christmas has transformed his features by a miracle of happiness. This is when he steps forward and sings:

> *I ain't even got a hot dog,*
> *I ain't never had a thing;*
> > *Christmas to me was never merry,*
> > *Nothing   extra-ordinary;*
> *But now I'm on the first plateau,*
> *And that is why I,*
> > *That is why I,*
> > *That is why I — sing!*

Now we shift to Scrooge. He is stuck in a traffic jam in a taxicab. Three panhandlers, representing the the past, present and future periphrastic, come in turn to revile him for his hard heart. He explains that he is reformed, has seen the error of his ways, and will now devote his every effort to Christmas love and joy.

I thought it would be nice to lay the next scene in Venice. You can do quite a bit with gondoliers in a chorale, and this offers a chance to show the international aspects of banking by having the Rialto in the background. Scrooge now runs up on the Bridge of Sighs (stage center) and throws his arms in the air and shouts, "Stop the music! Stop the music! I have been rejuvelized!"

His announcement is the greatest Christmas present the world has ever known. He says that he has just bought all the television networks, and has ordered all give-away shows off the air. Furthermore, he says, he has fired everybody in television who thinks he can improve on genius, and that in the future no musicals will be shown except those originally written as such, and then only upon order of the Supreme Court. As a finale for this happy scene, all the actors who ever appeared in *Bonanza* are kicked off the bridge into the water, and the gondoliers sing "Joy to the World."

Scrooge is now a national hero. Thousands jam the streets outside the studio and go wild with enthusiasm when he comes out. People who had always wanted to see something worthwhile on television have come from as far away as Montpelier, Vermont. Scrooge is stripped of his formal attire and thrust into a sooty red suit, a beard is clapped to his face, and he sings:

> *There surely is a Santy,*
> *As sure as I'm Durante —*

And as the tumultuous crowd bears him down Broadway the cameras fade out and we see Bob Cratchit walking slowly home to his fireless flat, weeping to himself. But Bob is no stranger to disappointment, and as he comes into his cheerless home he begins to hum "Deck the Halls" backwards, and he kindles a roaring blaze on the hearth — burning the books of Charles Dickens.

WHEN BELLS MEANT WORK

During every Christmas season, while the musicians are foisting upon us the non-Christmas music of "Jingle Bells," as if it were a fine old carol, I sit with my feet on the front of the kitchen range and wonder what "Jingle Bells" means to a jingleless generation. The last thing anybody could do these days would be to take a sleigh ride, yet the song seems to have great appeal.

[189]

For something that was never any fun anyway, the sleigh ride certainly has a strange hold on the popular fancy, and to make it synonymous with joy at the festive Yule season suggests a major deterioration of public intelligence. If all these people who sing "Jingle Bells" had to ride forth in a sleigh, behind a horse, they probably would not like it much — which is quite apart from the basic fact that "Jingle Bells" isn't Christmas music anyway.

Bells, as attached to the winter harnesses of horses, were nothing but a warning device. Wheels on wagons rattled and bumped, and you could hear horses tromping on summertime roads. But when snow fell the sounds of traffic were muted, and bells were added to warn folks. This being so, we have the intellectual right to ask why a foghorn or the gong on a trolley car didn't achieve some standing as Christmas music.

I would like to take, couple at a time, the members of the musicians' union for a nice, old-time ride in a set-over pung. O'er the fields we'd go, laughing all the way. They would find it is one thing to stroke violins and toot flutes in the comfort of the studio and concert hall, and quite another to jingle-jingle across country with your ears stiff and your fingers numb in your mittens. The set-over pung was the best thing we had for sleighing — it gave the one-horse sleigh a chance to ride on roads that were owned by teams. Sleighing was incidental, because our old winter roads were avenues of commerce and business was conducted on traverse runners with double-horse hitches.

So if you fared forth with a single horse with dash, zip, verve, gusto, hurraw and frivolity, as per "Jingle Bells," throwing caution to the winds, you would presently meet a logging rig with about four thousand feet of pine logs, a pair of chunks thrust forward into their collars, and a man on top who was not geared to your jollity even a little bit. This is when you jerked a rein, tried to get the sleigh runners out of the ice ruts, and tipped over. The bells on Bob-tail rang for fair, because Bob-tail usually took a fright and ran away.

The set-over pung had its whiffletree to one side, so the horse could tread in one of the hoof-paths but the runners would track with the team-sleds. It adjusted a single horse to the two-horse roadway. It was truly a wonderful invention, but it had certain disadvantages when you tried to turn out of the ruts. The horse made out fine, but the runners hung back. When this happened the happy revelers had a choice — they could get out on the up-side or they could get out on the down-side. The high-siders had farther to jump, but the low-siders would have all the middle-riders fall on them. On any jaunt with jingling bells,

[191]

along any country road when bells were jingling, the dashing sleigh would execute this maneuver at least every hundred yards, and a pung was upside down as often as not, and things were never so jubilant as the song conveys.

Some may not know about pungs. They were a "box sleigh," and were much better than the high-runnered things always pictured by Mr. Currier and Mr. Ives. Nobody used the word utilitarian then, but that's what a pung was. The word sleigh connotes a high check-rein and the lap-robe clique. In the pung you used a blanket, and usually a horse blanket, and if you put a lighted lantern by your feet you could attain some comfort. It was cheaper and easier to fix if you smashed it up, and being slung on low runners you didn't have so far to fall when it tipped.

One thing the glad carol-singing of "Jingle Bells" never considers is the nature of the horse. Around the farm in winter the road-horse didn't have much to do except stand in the barn and develop his personality. In the summer he raked hay and cultivated the tomatoes and could work off his disposition in the pasture when otherwise unoccupied. In winter he just stood and argued with his hay, and was called upon only for two chores. One was to take the eggs and butter to town once a week, and the other was to attend devotions on Sunday. Nobody ever looked forward to a pung ride, and the horse least of all. He hated bells. Bells meant he had to go to work. When he was backed out of the stall and into the shafters a deep mood of melancholy settled upon him, and he was inconsolable. He knew, for one thing, that the pung runners were frozen into the gravel and he would be expected to start them loose and then drag them a mile before they became smooth. He knew he would have to stand on the street while the dickering went on and on, or in the drafty shed behind the church while the sermon did likewise. No smart Maine farm horse had any love for pungs, and when you jingled a bell you made him sad.

When taking eggs, you had to put the lantern under the blanket, although humans could ride to church cold. You also had to be careful not to tip over too much. To avoid tipping over you kept a tight rein on the horse, and he didn't like that either. Besides, egg day was a week day, and farmers were hauling logs, hay and ice, so tipping over was much easier. On Sundays the traffic was reduced, but you had fine clothes on and didn't want to tip over then. The horse just never got a break in any of this. He hated sleigh rides.

When he was harnessed to the pung, the eggs were in place, the lantern bestowed, and everybody seated, the giddy-ap to the horse produced the wildest sensation in the history of mankind. Unless you've been seated in a pung on egg day, frozen to the ground, and have said giddy-ap to a knowing old Maine farm horse, you have never had the sensation of being jerked loose from your spine into the biting winter cold of a clear, sharp morning. The next five hundred yards were spent in reducing the horse to a respectable amble, which he also detested — because the longer it took, the longer he'd be away from his hay.

The trip back home after business or church was a wild ride, because we just let the horse go it. He'd turn out for traffic all by himself, and the pung would slat around in the air behind him like a short-tailed kite in a March wind. We'd hide down under the blankets, or robe on Sunday, and hang onto the lantern and hope for the best.

The sweetest sound jingling bells ever made was the silence that fell over the countryside when the horse pulled up by the back steps. He would turn and look back, and seem to count the passengers who alighted. One of them, he knew, would lead him to the barn, unhitch the pung so it could freeze in again, take off his harness, and let him head back into his stall. The rest of us would go into the house, blow out the lantern, and get thawed out.

Laughing all the way, indeed. A sleigh ride was a dangerous, frigid, unnerving, unpleasant, yek! torment of Ye Goode Olde Days, and if the musicians would stop playing and singing about it I would be the first to thank them.

A SNEEZE FROM MISS ALDRICH

"Tell me what a man reads," said my friend Julius Jenkins the other afternoon, ". . . and I'll tell you what he is." You may think you heard this before somewhere, but nothing ever becomes final until Jule says it, and for present purposes the remark may be considered original. Anyway, this past summer my old high school class had a reunion, and they passed the hat during the picnic to come up with two hundred and fifty dollars, which they gave to the principal to buy new books for the new library in the new school building.

I have just received from him a list of his purchases, with price of each, and by applying the Julius Jenkins rule I think I can see what a high school is like nowadays.

The principal, in buying this list of books, appears to have spent twenty dollars more than the donation, but he explains this by saying that some of the books are "approved" by the National Defense Act and there will be a subsidy on these and he will get back more than the twenty dollars. Those of us who have been told that federal assistance implies no federal control may care to ponder on this and notice the ingenious and subtle way Washington has of persuading school principals about which books to buy. Indeed, some of us may be alarmed that federal control of education is present before it was enacted. I gather the heavy purchase of physics books, with token attention to the liberal arts, is thus explained.

We had no school library when I was a student there. The manual training (now industrial arts) boys had made a plain pine book stand between two radiators on the wall, and it held a certain collection of "reference works" which we were encouraged to consult; and this was the nearest we came to a library in the schoolhouse itself. There was a picture encyclopedia which had the tantalizing thoroughness of offering everything except what you wanted to know. There was a collection of dictionaries — Webster's, and then a French-English, a German-English, a Latin-English. The rest was Stoddard's Lectures, and those that wouldn't fit into what was left of the shelves were up on the windowsill.

If research or curiosity took us beyond that, we went to the town library, which was in a Carnegie building and was run by a self-perpetuating committee of local businessmen whose erudition was not immense. This library was not attuned to school purposes, and nobody ever thought of coordinating, but luckily it had a librarian who was kind and loving, one who welcomed the student. Her name was Annette Aldrich, and I owe her a great deal. She introduced me to Mother West Wind; she introduced me to Bill Nye; she introduced me to Aristotle — and she patiently assisted when I came in to look things up for school. "Some of Shakespeare isn't worth reading," she told me once, and wisdom like that is priceless. Miss Aldrich earned less, as librarian, than the janitor of the library.

She was "Miss" Aldrich to the town, daughter of a seafaring ancestry that obviously fitted her for this work. She presided. That is the word for what Miss Aldrich did. Her desk was regal, and she sat on her throne. Noblesse oblige. Her greatest problem was the stringency of funds for new books, and her second was the committee's authorization to spend what she did have. They were respectable and trustworthy men, and they were going to buy only respectable and trustworthy books. The annual appropriation at town meeting included funds for heat and light, rebinding old veterans, the janitor's salary, and Miss Aldrich's stipend, as well as books. So not oftener than twice a year Miss Aldrich would receive a wooden crate from a wholesaler, the janitor would open it for her, and she would catalog and install a dozen or so new titles. They would stay on the New Books shelf until the next box arrived. You can see that Miss Aldrich was strongest in the old books department.

The scholar prying into the past would stand before her desk and state his case, she would think a moment and tap the desk with that lead pencil librarians have with a date-stamp attached to it for marking cards, and she would say, "Hm-m-m, yes..." She would walk behind the shelves and pick down a book and nod at it, and then she always did a most wonderful thing.

She would open the book and then slam it shut with a resounding slap that would make the people reading magazines at the tables jump. This would burst out a great cloud of erudite and sapient dust, which would billow and bulge all along the aisle, and which prompted Miss Aldrich to let fly an old bruiser of a sneeze. Miss Aldrich was forever a lady, but when she sneezed on book dust she gave it all she had. If Miss Aldrich sneezed we knew we were well back beyond the memory of man, in the limbo of history, where things were true and wonderful and important because they were old and made Miss Aldrich sneeze.

And every time Miss Aldrich found us books for our school work, and stamped them with the little thing on the end of her lead pencil, she would add at least one book of her own selection and say, "And this one is for fun . . ."

When I peeled a five-spot off my philanthropist's roll last summer and dropped it into the school library fund, I guess I had memories like Miss Aldrich in mind. I was not thinking of a year's subscription to *Hot Rod* magazine or books named *Big Molecules, Earth Science, Elements of the Universe,* and *Automotive Maintenance & Trouble Shooting.* I was certainly not thinking of titles which gain importance because of government refunds.

There was a propaganda value to Miss Aldrich. She nudged us carefully and intentionally into directions she thought were proper. She was a brainwasher, all right enough. She had us reading things by the transients — Dickens and Mark Twain and Poe and Hawthorne and a batch of other oddities now unlisted in the new school library. I doubt if I could make a principal understand that one sneeze from Miss Aldrich was a rich experience, worth more than five dollars.

LIKENESS AND DIS-LIKENESS

We have a manufacturing plant here in town that is affiliated with one of the bigger industrial combines in the country, and I stopped in the other day to say something to a friend who works there, and I stumbled on twenty-four of our nation's youth taking a career examination. They had a room fixed up like a school, and here were these hopeful, bright-eyed young folks bent over the printed forms, competing busily, and they had a brisk doctor of philosophy holding a stopwatch. My friend explained that from this group certain talented ones would be selected to join the family — they'd be started along learning the business, and would eventually have positions of trust in the corporation. The prize was rich. Have you ever wondered how you'd make out if you went back and took an examination? The professor handed me a sheet, and in the faintly erudite surroundings of a textile mill office I began.

I didn't pass the thing, because I didn't finish it. I didn't bother to finish it. I studied it full of wonder at the methods now used to recruit textile executives. This test, they told me, was to show general mental awareness, perceptiveness and adaptability, and I said, "Of whom?" They said the candidates, and I said, "What about the professor?" This test, I quickly concluded, was giving no challenge to the hopefuls who were ploddingly completing it, but it was a great indication of the professor's standards of knowledge and judgment. He was evaluating possible textile leaders, but nobody was evaluating him. Who, nowadays, evaluates a doctor of philosophy?

There was absolutely no way, in the process of taking that examination, that a person could reveal his perceptiveness, awareness and adaptability. These would be the very last things in the world that a test of this sort could reveal.

All these students could do, to pass, was to set down the exact answers the maker of the test had predetermined as the correct replies. The only thing the test could possibly show would be the ability of the candidate to conform to the intellectually obvious, to guess the nature of the expected answer, and there was no chance for reasoning and discernment, no way to express the delicious vagaries of human differences. Indeed, the completed papers were so prepared that they could be corrected by a machine.

I paused at a question on the examination that said, "Circle the two objects most alike." Somebody who had no perceptiveness, awareness or adaptability to the rudiments of creative art had then drawn pictures of several items, to wit: an electric light bulb; a thermometer; an onion; a toggle wall switch for an electric circuit; a potted plant in flower, and a Yo-Yo. A Yo-Yo is one of those top-like toys the youngsters jerk on a string.

I liked this question very much, for it seemed to

call for some perceptiveness, awareness and even adaptability as I looked from drawing to drawing and tried to make the selection that would best qualify me as an executive for a woolen worsted mill. This would be the way Young America approaches its opportunities. Here is the revelation which proves a boy or girl is ready. What two objects are most alike?

I can tell you exactly what licked me with this question. It was the awful affluence of knowing altogether too much. I have always considered Aristotle the best teacher of many topics, and as I sat there I found myself turning to him. The Father of Logic, they call him, and he laid down some rules which would now be of much help. First, we must agree upon a meaning of "alike." Inasmuch as likeness is a logical term, we forthwith conclude that a lamp, thermometer, onion, switch, flower and Yo-Yo are not "alike," and that the professor's original assumption is in error. The next step is to adjust the terms, and agree upon those areas where they may, by logic, develop some likenesses within the values of the adjustment. Thus, as Aristotle explains, we come to the second division of logic, which has to do with quality and quantity, or — as we may construe it — the "like-ness" and "dis-likeness" of things.

Well, a thing is either B or not-B; either an onion

or not-onion; but if C is part of A, and also part of B, then A and B have joint qualities or quantities. We can now go back to the little drawings on the examination paper and consider.

Easiest was the onion and the lamp — they are both "bulbs."

But then I hesitated, because through the mental exercise of the consideration came a haunting wonder as to how this would "test" anybody for the textile business? There ought to be some semblence of purpose showing through. If my reasoned answer were correct, the thing was too feeble to make into an examination. At very best, all I had arrived at was a poor pun, and this is unworthy of doctors of philosophy and textile executives. At least there should be a better pun than that. So, while I was operating wholly within the art-form of classical logic, I found myself doing nothing more than looking for a pun which was big enough and good enough to be significant to American Industry.

How about the onion and the lily (assuming the potted plant to be a lily!)? They are botanical cousins; the onion is a liliaceous plant with a pungent, edible bulb. But a farmer would know that — why find it on a textile quiz? Maybe the potted plant is not a lily at all, but a coreopsis or a geranium. This artist isn't too good. If it be a lily, then we know that a lily toils not, neither doth it spin — so it is unlike a Yo-Yo. The lily, however, is a symbol of peace, because of its purity and the retiring situation in which it usually grows, and an electric light switch is a piece of equipment . . .

I decided, after using all I could remember of Aristotle, that there could be only one logical answer. I circled the thermometer and the Yo-Yo — because they both go up and down. Aristotle, I felt, would be proud of my selection. I supposed the professor, also, would appreciate my ability with pure deductive reasoning.

But he didn't twinkle at all. He looked at my answer and asked how I arrived at it, and said blankly, "The correct answer is the syringe and the lamp."

"The syringe?" I said.

"Yes," he said. "What you call a Yo-Yo — that's a rubber syringe with a tube on it. The syringe and the lamp are both bulbs."

"You know," I said, "I don't think you need textile executives after all. I think you need a new artist!"

I could see that the doctor of philosophy wasn't altogether happy about my being around, so I came away without finishing the examination, and that's why I am back on the farm instead of running a big mill for J. P. Stevens.

THE ERA OF SURVEYS

If'n I had a lot of money I think I'd set up a fancy foundation which would do authentic, objective, unbiased surveys and reports to counteract authentic, objective, unbiased reports now being done by fancy foundations that have a lot of money.

There is a great need for this. The American people are being surveyed and reported down to the last faint, fine whisper, and two excellent unbiased surveys have just come to me here and started me to thinking again. These have been done in the high name of academic accuracy, with great protestation of equanimity, and with the obvious finality that oblique language proves anything.

Both these reports have had acceptance because they were done at great expense by an esteemed authority — not because anybody has read them. I would have gladly written both for the price of one, but I am not an esteemed authority — even though I would probably have been a good deal more honest about my bias. And I find I'm a little bitter about this — we have amongst us a great many intelligent and informed people who can never be experts because they don't have any degrees. Our devotion to the professional surveyist discounts all these fine people, and we never have the benefit of their opinions and advice. And this is absurd, because I know about the clams.

Well, back along about the time of World War I our native Maine clam began to fall on evil days. Civilized effluvia of one kind or another began to cut him down in his youth, and as he became less and less frequent our legislators thought they ought to do something, and maybe pass a few clam laws. At that time legislation was effected without benefit of surveys, and the plain truth was that nobody knew much about clams. So there was this old fellow from down the coast who had been a clam warden and selectman, and now was in the state legislature, and he wrote a little paper that had in it everything he, or anybody else, knew about clams. He didn't know what doubletalk was, and he couldn't spell some of the hard words, but he worked the thing up and then he had it mimeographed and gave copies to his colleagues in the House and Senate. He was no expert, no Ph.D., no professor, no statistician — he was just an interested longshore duffer who happened to be concerned about clams and knew a little about them. And by chance a copy of his exegesis was tucked away in the Maine State Library, and it is still there.

Well, after that came the era of surveys. My friend Stanley Tupper, who later became a congressman, did a little campaigning for Burton Cross, and this proved to be a prophetic activity. When Burt was elected governor he appointed Stan as Commissioner of Sea and Shore Fisheries for the State of Maine, and thus Stan found out about survey grants. Every once in a while Stan's office would get word that a sum of money was available for a survey of some phase of commercial fisheries, and Stan noticed that his biologists, experts and statisticians always measured these grants by the length of time involved, and not by the subject. There would be money for three months, six months, a year — even if the topic could be exhausted in two days' study. The extent of the subject and its intellectual challenge had nothing to do with the duration — if the money was for two months, you made it last two months.

And Stan became entranced with the great attention paid to the clam. Stan is a longshore boy himself, and grew up fairly cognizant of clams, and the idea of periodic surveys of the clam amused him. A clam sits in the mud with his hands folded, as contemplative as Buddha, and inside his shell occupies complete seclusion. There is something about a clam which suggests that his activities and his thoughts are rightfully his own business, and that nature intended this. Is it not wonderful that the Latin word "clam" means "secretly, in private"? *Clam aliquem habere*, says

Terence. But anyway, every so often a new fund for a survey of the clam would come to Stanley's desk, and he would look it over and OK the vouchers.

After a time, during which Stan perused the output of his surveying naturalists, he detected a sameness to the clam surveys. Except for polysyllabic variations and periphrastic nuances, they all seemed to say just about the same thing. Except, that each succeeding survey referred to all previous ones in footnotes and appendices, and that the clam lore as it advanced was much like a snowball rolling up more of the same. He also found that whatever each surveyist added, he eventually referred to the definitive work on the subject — the report done so long ago by the old duffer down the coast who was not, and never claimed to be, a surveyist or an expert. After Stanley had perused a certain number of these high-priced modern surveys he went down into the State Library and hunted out the original.

He thus uncovered, you see, the technique of the survey. First research, and then evaluation. In the research you finally get back to the old duffer's mimeographed paper, follow its evaluations through the subsidized versions, and then sit down and type what you find. Stan says it takes three months, on the dot.

Of course, you have to finalize the thing in frames

of reference. Where the old duffer said clams were fetching thirty cents a peck, the researchist changes that to "current economic impact." And you notice that along about the time of Franklin D. Roosevelt the word "clams" was elevated to "bivalve mollusks."

But there is more to it. You are required to evaluate the conclusions according to the way the foundation that is paying you has decided to be unbiased. You have to keep the objectivity in the right direction. I have one wonderful unbiased survey here which was done by a team of objective surveyists on the proposal to make a National Park in the Allagash River wilderness. It turns out this team of surveyists never took the Allagash canoe trip. Then I have this other one that begins, "It goes without saying that municipal managers have been successful." The survey, we find, is an unbiased study about the success of municipal managers. It was financed objectively by a society of municipal managers. With clams, the researchist must bear in mind whether he is being unbiased for the Anti-Pollution League or for the Associated Industries. So, our great need at this time seems to be for independent surveys to offset other independent surveys. We need neutral scholarship on both sides.

COUNTRY MOUSE, CITY MOUSE

When the Supreme Court of the United States of America decided city people are important and ordered some changes made, it demoted us country bumpkins to second-rate citizens, and I urge that an antidiscrimination demonstration be launched at once. It is now or never, and if we don't assert ourselves we shall be undone forevermore. The ancient fable of the country mouse and the city mouse, once merely literary and open to contemplation, is now in the corpus juris and can be cited in court.

To begin with, I'd like to complain once more about parking meters. Every time one of us inferior people goes to the big city to spend a little money, thus contributing to urban prosperity, the first money we spend is a coin to gain temporary rental of a piece of the street. This does not please us, but we have nowhere to moan. Then on the following weekend we look up from our bucolic labors to see city people arriving in droves to park their automobiles for free all over the place and enjoy without charge the landscape and atmosphere.

If the cities are as wonderful as the Supreme Court seems to think, why do those lucky people who live

there leave the joys and pleasures to come out and inspect the miseries of the unwonderful countryside? To remove inequities, I want to see parking meters put up on every country lane and bypass. Proceeds to be devoted to a program of rural renewal we must shortly enact. If the favored cities are worthy of subsidized improvement, certainly the unfortunate farming areas deserve as much. Whatever the cities have, we want it!

In the name of "recreation" we've been obliged to do a number of things out here in the wilds to accommodate slumming urbanites. There should be a reciprocal program. I ought to be allowed to wickiup on Boston Common, or launch my dory in the pond at the Public Garden. I ought to be allowed to cut down an ulmus americanus right there in the heart of Boston so I could cook my simple country meals and save restaurant expenses. I guess I ought to be able to go in and see all the shows free.

Well, last summer I was perambulating my inferior domain, feeling bereft because I didn't have the advantages of metropolitan connections, and I came upon a city gentleman and his lady who were wrapped in deep contemplation. He had binoculars about two feet long, and he would look through them into the top of a spruce, and then he would pass them to her and she would look into the top of the spruce. "Whaddaya see?" I called cheerily, it never entering my head that I was a second-rate citizen. The gentleman unscrewed the device from his eyes, turned to look me over with patronizing detail, and said, "A red-eyed vireo!"

Maybe I imagined it, but I'm not so sure — he sounded as if he thought I wouldn't know what a red-eyed vireo is, since my shoes were not polished and I was not wearing a tie. Well, that's all right; but I wonder what that man would say if I drove up on his lawn sometime and left my automobile by the forsythia? I think this is the area where we country people must arise and demand equal opportunity.

And if the Supreme Court's general reasoning is correct, and I suppose we must accept it until "nature and nature's God" has pondered an appeal, I can't understand why we have all this pressure in the cities for wilderness preservation. If somebody out here decides to log off a woodlot he's been carefully growing for forty years, there comes a great outcry that he is ravaging public beauty, and the brutal ax must be restrained. If the countryside isn't important to the Supreme Court, what difference does it make to anybody else? So, now that the decision is on record, I suppose we'll hear no more about that. We know now that the intersection of Broadway and Forty-Second is what we really must preserve; that the traffic lights at Tremont and Boylston shine more meaningfully than any silvery moon o'er placid waters through the dark pines on the shores of yon lake. Idealest place for a new-day picnic would be a subway platform; maybe the foyer of the halls of justice.

Another point of reform would be the evacuation routes set up by Civil Defense. They would all have to be turned right around and run the other way. Civil Defense laid them out so, in time of peril, the favored and superior city people would be led right away from the good places, and out into the sticks, where things are not good enough. The court ruling shows us that if catastrophe accrues, it would be much more salutary to move all the farmers into the cities, where they can enjoy the advantages.

Well, just think what it would be like out here in the country if the population turned up; this is no place to cope with an emergency. The thing to do is to reverse all those signs, and at the first omen of disaster flock everybody under the shelter of the nice city. I, for one, shall lose no time — you'll see me coming in over the Mystic Bridge with my cow and chickens, cat in a basket, and the eager determination of a patriotic citizen to obey the Supreme Law of the Land. "Noblesse Oblige!" I shall say, and I shall settle in to enjoy the judicial benevolences of the city.

Funny thing, but I was talking to a red-eyed vireo just lately, and he said he wouldn't be around next summer. He's planning to stop off in Washington, D.C., and stay there to do some people-watching. He said above everything else, he wants to get a good look at a Supreme Court justice, or two.

EVER CATCH SHEEP?

Having intentionally dedicated a great part of my generous philanthropies to the sedentary philosophies, I was obliged to view with alarm the political contention that America is physically unfit and we must all get up on the bars and chin. Exercise doesn't appeal to me overmuch, and I was greatly shaken by the news that some school, somewhere, had dutifully responded to this national crisis and had trained the boys to take a wooden peg in each hand and walk right up a wall full of holes. I wonder if these boys could catch a sheep?

I hear on the radio that if I hurry I may yet get a tubular-steel gymnasium unit for my weakling children, with stamps, and save them from disgrace while advancing the President's program of muscular might. The truth is that my youngsters are a little past the push-up age, and can catch sheep.

My youngsters were never much on exercise, but

they could run in the woods and leap up and catch at the limb of a tree and hoist themselves up to shake beechnuts or look in a crow's nest. They never got any training at push-ups, but they know how to lie flat on their bellies at the pasture spring and get a drink of water and then get back up to run again. They never knew what the rings were, but they could hang onto a scaffling rope and swing to the ground mow. And they knew how to catch sheep. Do you suppose any of those Washington sycophants who trudged twenty tedious miles to prove they were fit could catch a sheep?

I can still catch a sheep, and I haven't had a lick of exercise in a long time. If the head Olympic coach took one look at me he'd shake his head in dismay. Catching sheep is not on the Olympic list, and he wouldn't know that a good sheep-catcher could take the ski jump and the marathon in the morning, and then come back in the afternoon and sew up the de-cathlon. I suppose the reason they don't give a laurel crown for sheep-catching at the Olympics is because it would be too much strain on the athletes.

A lot of farm jobs are much the same. Like getting a barrel of vinegar up from down cellar on a plank. You don't see them doing that at the Olympics. Or setting a hogs' trough right side up while three half-grown sows and a barrow are standing on it, squealing for dinner. Or getting the bit into an elderly horse who had just decided to take the day off.

Nope. If this nation needs exercise, I recommend that the Secretary of Welfare get some sheep and turn them loose in populated sections with a prize of durable value to each citizen who catches one. We'd be trimmed down to a pinpoint-fit nation in two weeks. We'd have the greatest per capita national fitness since the Amazons. There is nothing that contributes to agility of coordination and muscular stability like a breachy sheep that hasn't been caught yet.

I know because I've seen it, but you take a young man who is virtually without proper exercise, and has only to grain the hens, water the young stock, fill the woodboxes, walk two miles to school and back, pick up the eggs, split kindlings and churn, and if you speak to him patriotically and suggest that he ought to do a few push-ups so the nation will be safe from decay, you will notice a lack of zeal on his part. He will appear reluctant. But if somebody yells and says a sheep is loose in the green peas, that boy will leap to exercise obligingly and become a useful citizen.

To such a boy, some of the track and field records seem smallish. He can high-jump a ten-foot fence, leap a twenty-foot brook, and do a hundred yards through the puckerbrush in three seconds, and with his hi-cut boots on. I tell you, I'm all for sheep-catching as the basic exercise for national security.

I'm talking about Maine sheep, of course — which are different. We've never had great flocks of sheep here, with trained dogs to handle them. There is a reason for this, and it was a taxation arrangement. The cagey old Founding Fathers observed that it took just about so many sheep to keep an early Maine subsistence family in wool and mutton, so they exempted the first ten sheep from taxes. High-minded government economists who like to debate the impact of unfavorable taxes on business and industry ought to take notice that nobody much in Maine ever has more than ten sheep. This is true even though sheep do very well in Maine, the fiber is good and the fleeces will grade out well and profitably. Sheep might have become a leading farm item in Maine, but they were taxed at ten, and ten is about all a farm has.

So we never made a big thing of sheep; they were extra and we fenced them. They usually ran with other cattle. We made pets of them. And if one got over the fence and was disturbing the gardens, he had to be caught. Sheep are followers by nature, and if one got out they all would. So we tried to determine the leader and we'd put a yoke on him, or her. Often all this trouble with sheep led to decisions not to have any at all. Farms would go five and six years without sheep, but then you'd have some more for a while. I figure I've had sheep seven times, and six times I haven't.

Sheep are short-winded. They can outduck, outrun, outmaneuver, outguess and outsmart you amazingly, and if an inexperienced sheep-chaser gives them any pause, or tries to sneak up on them, or schemes strategy, they can keep loose all day. But if you simply larrup after them, never hesitating a moment, keeping at full tilt every minute, o'er hill and dale and fence and swamp, a sheep will give up before you do. It's you or him. How long it takes is his option, but you will win if you don't stop. And after you have won, and yoked him and fixed the fence, and somebody comes by and says you are physically unfit and need exercise, a great doubt wells up in you and you find yourself resisting any suggestion that you do some push-ups, or chin yourself — or take a peg in each hand and climb a wall full of holes.

THE VIRTUES OF BRAND X

The other day, some waggish bent welling up in me beyond resistance, I asked Bill Leach, my grocer, where he kept his harsh, ordinary, wash-day detergent. You know, the one that all the others are better than. It doesn't do anything, and I have always wondered why it remains on the market. I found out it isn't on the market. You can't buy it. Bill didn't have a single box of Brand X in his store.

Then Bill lowered his voice and told me about the Red Stripe. He had an item that came in a blue box, and one day a vast national advertising program told everybody that a Red Stripe had been added. When Bill opened his next shipment, he got the same old blue box, but a Red Stripe had been printed across it. Since he still had quite a supply of the old blue boxes on hand, he arranged his shelves with some of each, side by side. Then he noticed that the women took the boxes with the Red Stripe, and made a wonderful American distinction between the same thing. He says in his entire experience with this kind of merchandising he has never seen any effort by the public to figure things out.

Then I asked him if he had any ordinary fly spray. The kind that has no penetration power and does not work with residual effect. The kind that does not seek the bugs out where they are. He said he was fresh out of that, too.

So I asked him if his salt pork is saturate, polysaturate, or non-saturate, and just then a woman was going by pushing a cartful of groceries and she heard what I said. She had been confident as she made her purchases, secure in the serenity of advertised assurances, and all at once we could see that a doubt had been raised in her mind. Mists had been rolled away, and Shining Truth stood revealed. All at once she realized that she, too, had no notion about the status of salt pork.

You can't get an ordinary floor wax, either. I asked for an ordinary floor wax, and the clerk tiering up dogfood said, "What, sir?" I told him I wanted the old-fashioned kind that turns yellow, the kind that streaks and is sticky, and which won't harden to a luster-gloss that lasts longer. "I have seen it advertised on television," I said. The boy looked mildly puzzled for a moment, but he got over it. "We don't carry that brand," he said.

Don't let me appear to be belittling. The polyunsaturate inexpensive spread is really a fine product, and if pressed I would gladly give it an unqualified endorsement. It is wonderful stuff, and not long ago I saw a dramatized demonstration that would make an excellent commercial on the networks. Flats Jackson owns a little log-cabin camp up on Wobbler Stream which he rents out during the summer and fall to "sports," or as they are now called, recreationists. It isn't much of a camp, but it's close to good fishing and hunting, and he doesn't have any trouble keeping it occupied. There isn't much upkeep to it, but every fall, after the season, Flats goes up and fixes things for winter. He checks the roof, hangs the bedding on wires, ties the door open so the bears won't break it in — and he greases the stove.

This stove is a little biscuit-baker, with a wide hearth for putting up feet, and it has an oven door on both sides. It is a bilateral stove. It gets dampish along Wobbler Stream, so to keep this stove from rusting during the winter and spring Flats always carries in a little bottle of engine oil for it. In the late spring, when the first angler touches off the first fire of the season, this oil burns off and makes a stench and a smoke you wouldn't believe, but the treatment keeps the stove looking nice. So this fall Flats asked me if I'd like to ride up with him while he set the camp to rights, and I went along. We'd had some snow, so we had to walk the last half-mile, and we folded the bedding and arranged the dishes, and took down the stovepipe, and then Flats remembered that he had forgotten to bring his little bottle of oil.

Making-do is a virtue, so I said, "How about this stuff?" It was a pound package of a polyunsaturate inexpensive spread. I don't think it was a new kind. I think it was an old kind that the new ones are better than. One of the sporting parties had brought it in but hadn't used it. It doesn't need ice to keep it respectable, so it was left on the shelf by the sink. I broke the package open, and Flats and I greased the stove with it. It worked fine. Didn't crumble, and it covered well. It didn't give the stove that slick, oily appearance, either, but left it with a relaxed tone much in keeping with the remote wilderness location.

When Flats went in that following spring to open the camp for his first guests, he said it looked as if the bears had lapped the stove some, but not too much, and that when he touched off the first fire there arose a mild, mellow aroma that was entirely pleasing. He said he would never grease a stove again with anything else. It is the only polyunsaturate stove in the whole State of Maine.

BOUNTIES OF BENEFICENT NATURE

It hasn't been mentioned too much in the important dispatches from the crucial news-making spots of our troubled world, so I guess the really important people haven't paused to take notice that the wild field strawberries are in season. They are, and we have just had our annual shortcake under the trees on the lawn. It happened to be the same day the House passed the International Trade Agreements of 1962, and Huntley-Brinkley covered that closely as an item of great moment which, too, shall pass. They did not exert sufficient discernment to spend any time on our strawberry shortcake, and this is the measure of their worth.

Of all the bounties of a beneficent nature, the wild strawberry rides close to the top of the list. It might have pleased a kindly chance to have given us wild strawberries as big as plums, or to have caused them to grow on trees, but such was not the outcome.

Instead, this magnificent boon comes to us tiny and shy, hiding in the grass, the wealth of its fragrance and delight tied up in a size so miniature it takes at least eighteen to make a dozen. Of all the odors, aromas and flavors of a varied universe, none is so smallishly immense as that of the wild strawberry.

True, the International Trade Agreements Act of 1962 was carefully planned over a long time, and numerous experts cogitated, but all I was doing that day was cultivating my tomatoes. This is traditional; they go together. A lot of country things go together, like apple blossoms and trout. When the grapevines have run out their new shoots so they need to be tied, the bees will swarm. When an old mother duck comes off the nest to brag, it is time to stake the delphiniums. And when tomatoes are ready for cultivating, strawberries are ripe.

You can smell them. No rainbow in a poet's sky ever caused a heart to leap up as will the heart whose nose has just smelled wild field strawberries on a Maine morning. I smelled them as I drove up to scratch the tomatoes, right from the tractor seat, and I smelled them all along the way by patches. They grow by patches, and they can be different, patch by patch. Some patches give stubby little berries close to the ground and deep red and sweet and juicy. Some have longer stems. Some berries are pear-shaped and get no more than pink. They're all good, all wild, and they all help fill the dish.

Except that I used my hat. Dishes and baskets were at the house, but I had a hat with me. So I finished the tomatoes, which were looking well, and I parked the tractor by the fence and hunkered down to begin.

I can understand why a lot of people say such-and-such is just as good. Huntley-Brinkley wouldn't pick strawberries. It's a lot easier and quicker to grab a couple of baskets of cultivated strawberries at the store, or to reach a couple of boxes of frozen ones from the freezer, and then talk yourself into pre-ferring them. Compromising saves the American people a lot of effort. But I think, deep down, people really know better. They say cultivated strawberries are just as good, but what they mean is that they aren't going to go out and get some real ones.

And, of course, they're right. In a minimum-wage society wild strawberries aren't worth gathering. In the International Trade Agreements Act of 1962 there isn't one word about field strawberries. But in the pleasant summer afternoon, on your knees in the tall grass, with the tomatoes cultivated, and a bull bobolink combing you out over property rights, strawberries have a way of making liars out of the great speakers of truth. The world is a big place, and important, and the more you think about it there in the grass, the more you realize that hardly anybody knows where you are. Indeed, Congress itself could walk by twenty feet away and never know you were there! A man could walk by with his mind on all manner of important things, and he wouldn't see you for the grass.

He wouldn't, but somehow a bumblebee bumbling by discovers you. He does a double-take and comes back to look at you again, probably wondering what you're doing there with no hat on. He makes a few passes around your ears, real friendly like, and then gives up and buzzes on. It's none of his affair. And not quickly, and not easily, but in due time the hat is full.

I carried them, that day, to the house, and dumped them in a bowl on the table. She came over and looked at them and said, "Oh, Boy!" She didn't say Oh-Boy at Huntley-Brinkley that evening. She leaned over and sniffed them — a long, grateful, discriminating sniff that appraised the full fragrance and assessed it in all its lovely parts. "Is there anything," she said, "that smells like a bowl of wild strawberries!"

I said, "Of course there is."

She said, "Well, I'd like to know what it is!"

I said, "The inside of my hat."

So she brought out some buttermilk and het the oven, and began hulling berries — a miserable job one does willingly when there are ten thousand other miserable jobs you wouldn't do at all. The buttermilk shortcakes browned, the berries proved to be exactly the right size, and we sat there under the tree on the lawn and ate every last smack just as Congress took the vote.

THE GOULD-WINDSOR CORRESPONDENCE

A great many people who knew I was going to write to the Queen of England have asked me how I made out. The reason they knew I was going to write was that I went around asking people how you address a letter to a reigning monarch. It seems that around the State of Maine nobody much does this, and almost everybody said, "I don't know — 'Dear Queen,' I guess." I hoped that when the Queen received my letter she would treasure it not only for its contents, but because it represented quite an achievement in research. We are bucolically oriented here, and in both distance and attitude remote. None of us has communicated so high since John Cabot sent back a quotation on salt cod.

What I had to say to Her Majesty is, of course, a private matter, and I suppose it is not strictly my place to divulge the subject of our communications. Let me say, merely, that I came upon a smidgen of intelligence which I thought she would like to know, and which if I remained silent she was not likely to encounter. I owe no allegiance to her, politically, and I acted only out of decency and courtesy — I would hope that if the Queen came upon something I should know she would get in touch. The fact that our social strata are divergent should not, I hope, set up a barrier.

I found out, right away, that it would be best not to noise this around too much. I found this out when I mentioned it first to my wife and said, "How do you address a letter to the Queen?" "Why don't you just call her up?" she said. "The mails are so slow." Even my wife couldn't accept that I wanted to write a letter to the Queen. "I mean it," I said. "I want to write to the Queen. How do I start the letter?"

"It all depends on how well you know her," she said. "Why don't you just say 'Dear Bess'?" I think this is partly Yankee frivolity and partly the American spirit, or may be jealousy — but it isn't any help. If I write to my Senior United States Senator I say, "Sen. Margaret Chase Smith, Dear Margaret." She calls me John. But somehow the personal touch that goes with grass roots down East politics doesn't seem right. I knew very well I shouldn't say, "Queen Elizabeth, Dear Queen."

Getting no help at home, I then asked a few of my know-it-all friends, discreetly, of course, "How do I write to the Queen of England?" Without exception, every one of them replied the same, "What do you want to write to her about?" They seemed hurt when I said it was a personal thing.

Our farm library, while useful for many things, didn't help any. One book dismissed the whole epistolary art by telling me to say, "Dear Sir or Madame as the case may be." I couldn't quite imagine what that would sound like in the palace. Another book told me there is no informal way of addressing a reigning monarch, but didn't tell me what the formal way would be. It told me how to address the clergy, judiciary, ambassadors, cabinet members and the President. I haven't been writing to any of these for quite some time, on principle, and most of them have been equally sparing of word to me.

True, I knew kings and queens exist only in the

objective case and in indirect discourse, and that when they speak they say "We." But to a non-subject, in a distant land, the refinements of this are hard to come by. Possibly the Queen would permit a little latitude to a colonial, and particularly somebody from Maine. I found out, of course, that being formal with a Queen is about as cold as an Isle au Haut clam, and although it seemed at odds with my warm intentions I began, properly enough, "To the Queen's Most Gracious Majesty ..." "May it please Your Majesty," I wrote. And when I took the letter into my post office and Bill Moulton looked at it, he said, "Whoops!"

"That's all right," I said. "When Her Britannic Majesty replies, kindly let me know."

I am bound to report, however, that the Gould–Windsor correspondence was a dismal flop. The Queen, personally, did not reply. In revealing this, I must now explain why I wanted to write in the first place. I hate to, because even though I was soundly rebuked by Her Majesty, I still defer to her position and prestige. I would prefer she make any public announcements concerning us, but this doesn't suit the sequence of this report. The simple fact is that I had an aunt who was about to observe her hundredth birthday anniversary on Prince Edward Island, which is one of the British dominions beyond the sea, and I had heard that the Queen customarily sends a congratulatory telegram to any subject who attains a century. I worried lest the Queen wouldn't know this without my informing her. That's all there was to it. I didn't want to be poky, but I saw an opportunity to keep the worthy customs of the Crown intact. I was only trying to be nice.

Probably the real reason I wrote the Queen is that so many nice people write to me. If I use a booming whom where I should have who-ed, letters arrive from all over the world from lovely people who want me to know they care. I am grateful for this, and I understandably transferred all this to my relationships with the Queen. I thought she would like to know. It seemed to me that if, perchance, she didn't know about my aunt from other channels, her gratitude would be tremendous. All I really said was that my aunt was about to become a centenarian, but I hoped this would have double importance because it came from a plain United Stateser who had no ax to grind other than polite respect.

Alas, as they say, and lackaday.

When my reply came it was from The Private Secretary, who responds anonymously. It was a printed form with blanks to be filled in, with ink, and when the blanks were all filled in by The Private Secretary the gist was that they begged to inform me in a most diffident manner that I had pulled one whoop-de-doo of a boo-boo.

It seems that a matter of this kind is not brought to Her Majesty's attention in this abrupt and boorish fashion. It seems there are proper channels "for all such communications which it is desired to bring to the notice of the Queen." It seems that what I should have done, if I had possessed a single ounce of sense, was to get in touch with the Governor General of Canada, who would then have paddled along the proper channels, and once he was satisfied that my gracious aunt actually was one hundred, he would in due form, and with proper poo-bah, proceed. His Excellency would recommend to the Queen that the cable be dispatched, and only then would she oblige. I have this in writing from Buckingham Palace, and at precisely that point I reluctantly brought an end to the Gould-Windsor letters.

A RITUALISTIC THING

As spring approaches every year I find myself doing a ritualistic thing — I stand in the sunny dooryard and look off across the valley and ponder on the beginnings. What I see is a new frontier, for here the ancestor met the challenge of his own time and established the comforts and pleasures we now enjoy. I like to dwell on the way things were then.

This ancestor moved back from the coast where the fisheries had settled into a humdrum. Timber was the new attraction. He made arrangements with a crown proprietor, and at nineteen years of age sought his new frontier in the very first westward migration from salt water. That he moved a mere ten miles is unimportant; he was as remote and isolated as if he had gone ten thousand.

He came up here on the hill in the spring of the year. The corn snow was crumbling in the woods, and his first farming activity would be to tap the rock maples. Not on any commercial scale as it has been done in later times, but out of the necessity for sweetening for his own home use. He had none of the equipment we now have. He sawed chunks off pine logs, split them, and gouged out the halves into rough wooden receptacles. He sawed limbs off the maples, and as the sap dripped from the stubs he caught it in his bowls, reducing it by fire in the only metal kettle he had. When the snow had retreated, there was sugar enough for the year ahead. His first gross farm product!

The simple brush lean-to he made by laying spruce boughs against his wagon gave way to a pole shelter with a sailcloth top. With their two babies, he and his wife were to live in that until they got ready to put up a log cabin — and to hasten that achievement his wife helped chop logs.

I know, laying up a log cabin is sometimes depicted in modern movies as a community chore — everybody turns out and helps, and then there is a gay feast spread under sheltering trees. But by the time the ancestor came to lay his up, his wife was concerned with motherhood for the third time, and as he looked about to see who could help him with the logs he found only himself. So he rigged ropes and chains and poles, and by the same devices the tens of thousands of slaves used at the Pyramids he fitted the great punkin-pine logs into place. He had to teach his oxen to respond to vocal commands first, so he could be boosting while they hauled away.

He made the roof with poles and shakes. The soft-grained pine logs of that time were ideal for shakes. Chunks sawed from the log were stood on end, and straight, smooth pieces were split with a shingle-maker's tool called a frow. You had to know just how to set the frow, and how to strike it, and shake-making wasn't altogether easy. In later years the ancestor became known as the best shake-maker in the quadrangle, and later-comers paid him to make their shakes.

He had no nails, so he attached these shingles to

the roof with poles that held them down. Each row shed to the one below, and at the top he neatly fitted on his "ridgepole." In my ancestor's time a ridgepole really was a ridgepole, and not saddleboards. The trick came in fitting this pole with an ax until it was tight. It was late in the fall that he had this roof over their heads and could give his attention to a chimney.

He had no way to shape or cut stones, and he had no bricks. He had no mortar. But all summer he had kept an eye out, and whenever he saw a rock with potential he would come toting it to his pile. He now rigged a gantry, stood up a ladder, and he began going up and down that ladder to fit the stones together into a fireplace and flue. There was chill in the Maine air before he came to the "owl stone," a flat rock that fitted on top and was intended to keep birds from coming down the chimney.

So, that first summer, he built his home. He also arranged shelter for his animals and constructed certain conveniences such as stools and tables. The floor of his home was dirt, but he had some fur rugs. The beds, sumptuously comfortable with the natural spring of balsam boughs, and fragrant beyond desire, were on a half-loft under the roof, gained by a ladder. Here, on a moonlit night in late November, their third child was born, and they settled in to wait out the long Maine winter. It was going to be bleak, frugal and lonesome. But they had plenty of fuel, ample food, and a great desire to see springtime again.

And, as it always does, the winter at last began to break up. They came to the "Hill of March." The sun was holding higher in the sky and there were southerly winds that blew up fresh with rain. Down under the corn snow he could hear the trickle of melting water. This year he could really tap the maples, because he had whittled some spiles to cheat the tedium of winter. He had some better bowls, and more of them. He had a field chopped and ready to be burned and planted, and he knew now that winters to come would be easier to manage. From now on things would take shape, and there would be increasing comfort and even luxury.

So, I find myself standing about where he used to, this time of year, looking at things and reflecting on the then and the now. I wonder if, in his twentieth year, he looked ahead, maybe, to about the same age I am now, and figured he'd be pretty well fixed. There was no reason he shouldn't — you couldn't ask for much better prospects than he had! The new frontier, to him, was his own dooryard, and the key to all the future was the sharp ax he held in his own hand. There was nothing nebulous or symbolic about it — he was surrounded by it, and it was all his. And

I'm sure, as he stood in the morning and looked off, that he had some realization of how fortunate he was in his dreams, ambitions — and possessions.